AMERICA'S GODLY HERITAGE

David Barton

Aledo, Texas
www.wallbuilders.com

Additional materials available from:
WallBuilders
P. O. Box 397
Aledo, TX 76008
(817) 441-6044
www.wallbuilders.com

Cover Painting:
The Granger Collection, New York

Library of Congress Cataloging-in-Publication Data
261.7
Barton, David
America's Godly Heritage.
Aledo, TX: WallBuilder Press
64 p.; 21 cm.
Endnotes included.
A transcript of the video and audio by the same title.
ISBN 10: 0-925279-29-3
ISBN 13: 978-0-925279-29-3
1. Religion and politics   2. Christianity and politics   I. Title

Printed in the United States of America

America's Godly Heritage

Does America really have a Godly heritage? It definitely does, and abundant proof of this fact is available in tens of thousands of historic documents. In fact, copious evidence is readily visible in a consideration of the individuals and incidents in and around just one small building: Independence Hall in Philadelphia – the birthplace of American liberty and the origin of American constitutional government.

INDEPENDENCE HALL

In that building on July 2, 1776, the Founding Fathers in the Continental Congress voted to approve a complete separation from Great Britain; on July 4th, they approved the Declaration of Independence; and on July 8th, they carried the Declaration outside Independence Hall, read it to the assembled crowd, and then rang the Liberty Bell. Most citizens assume that the famous bell derives its name from the fact that it rang when America announced its liberty, but such is not the case. It is called the Liberty Bell because of the Biblical inscription from Leviticus 25:10 emblazoned around it:

> Proclaim liberty throughout the land, to all the inhabitants thereof.

Next door to Independence Hall is Carpenters' Hall – the building in which the first American Congress met. In 1774, forty of America's leading statesmen

CARPENTERS' HALL

from across the thirteen colonies (including luminaries such as Patrick Henry, John Adams, George Washington, John Jay, Samuel Adams, and many others) met in that Hall to prepare for the approaching conflict with Great Britain. That Congress opened with prayer, but according to historical records, it was not a superficial prayer like might be prayed in a public gathering today. To the contrary, it was a profound time of prayer led by the Rev. Jacob Duché, a local minister from nearby Christ Church.

Christ Church is where many of the Founding Fathers worshipped, and where seven signers of the Declaration of Independence are buried: Benjamin Franklin, Benjamin Rush, James Wilson, Francis Hopkinson, Joseph Hewes, and George Ross. So many Founders worshipped at Christ Church that around 1910, a famous stained glass window (now called "Patriot's Window") was added, showing many of the Founders and famous Americans attending church there, including:

FIRST PRAYER IN CONGRESS IN CARPENTERS' HALL

- Robert Morris and his family (Morris was one of the elite group of six Founding Fathers who signed both the Declaration of Independence and the Constitution);

- George Washington and his wife, Martha;

- Alexander Hamilton (a signer of the Constitution and an author of the *Federalist Papers*);

- Dr. Benjamin Rush (a signer of the Declaration and the "Father of Public Schools Under the Constitution");

- Joseph Hopkinson (a federal judge and a constitutional attorney who was the son of Declaration signer Francis Hopkinson);

- Francis Hopkinson and his family (Hopkinson was a signer of the Declaration and an early federal judge appointed by President George Washington);

- John Penn and his family (Penn was the grandson of Pennsylvania founder William Penn and was a governor of Pennsylvania before the Revolution); and

- Benjamin Franklin and his daughter, Sarah (Franklin is another of the six who signed both the Declaration and the Constitution; he was also Governor of Pennsylvania).

PATRIOTS' WINDOW WITH THE CONGREGATION WORSHPPING IN 1790. IN THE FRONT ROW IS ROBERT MORRIS AND HIS CHILDREN, WHITE AND HARRISON; IN THE AISLE TO THE LEFT IS FRANCIS HOPKINSON AND HIS SON; IN THE SECOND ROW IS GEORGE AND MARTHA WASHINGTON, ALEXANDER HAMILTON, AND BETSY ROSS; IN THE THIRD ROW IS BENJAMIN RUSH AND JOSEPH HOPKINSON; IN THE FOURTH ROW IS JOHN PENN AND HIS FAMILY, AND IN THE FIFTH ROW IS BENJAMIN FRANKLIN AND HIS DAUGHTER, SARAH

On September 6, 1774, the pastor of this church, the Rev. Jacob Duché, came to Carpenters' Hall to open the first American Congress with prayer. [1] Of that time of prayer, John Adams reported:

> [Rev.] Duché, unexpectedly to everybody, struck out into an extemporary prayer which filled the bosom of every man present. I must confess I never heard a better prayer. . . . with such fervor, such ardor, such earnestness and pathos, and in language so elegant and sublime for America [and] for the Congress. . . . It has had an excellent effect upon everybody here. [2]

Silas Deane, also a member of that Congress, declared that it was "a prayer . . . worth riding one hundred mile to hear" [3] (i.e., that it was worth spending three days on horseback to arrive in time for that prayer), and that as a result of that prayer, "even Quakers shed tears." [4] Additionally, the Congress read from four chapters in the Bible that morning, and as John Adams reported to his wife, Abigail, one particular chapter especially impacted the group:

> I never saw a greater effect upon an audience. It seemed as if Heaven had ordained that Psalm to be read on the morning. . . . I must beg you to read that Psalm. . . . [Read] the 35th Psalm to [your friends]. Read it to your father. [5]

(Numerous other delegates also commented on that profound time of prayer and Bible study. [6])

After meeting the first year in Carpenters' Hall, the Continental Congress then moved to Independence Hall, which served as its home for the next several years. From the Continental Congress came many of our famous Founding Fathers, great national leaders, military generals, and U. S. Presidents. In fact, America's first four Presidents all served in Congress in Independence Hall.

An interesting anecdote involving one of those four occurred in 1777. John Adams of Massachusetts, who went on to become America's second president, became close friends with Dr. Benjamin Rush of Philadelphia while serving in Congress, and both signed the Declaration of Independence. Dr. Rush, known as the "Father of American Medicine," had been appointed by Congress as the Surgeon General of the Continental Army, and in 1777, he traveled to the different battlefield hospitals, helping the wounded and monitoring the medical conditions before returning to Congress.

At that point in the American Revolution, things were not going particularly well: America was losing many more battles than it was winning. With such a bleak prospect of success, Dr. Rush leaned over to John Adams and candidly asked if he thought that America could actually win the Revolution. Adams' answer was clear and unequivocal. He confidently replied:

Yes! – if we fear God and repent of our sins! [7]

This account, unknown to most Americans today, was characteristic of the tone so often manifested within Independence Hall. In fact, during the American Revolution the Continental Congress issued fifteen separate prayer proclamations calling the nation to times of prayer and fasting, or prayer and thanksgiving (depending on the circumstances at that time); [8] those proclamations were characterized by overtly Christian language.

In 1787, Independence Hall served as home to the body that eventually produced the U. S. Constitution. Yet, few today know that virtually every one of the fifty-five Founding Fathers who framed the Constitution were members of orthodox Christian churches [9] and that many were outspoken evangelicals. [†]

† Many assume that the term "evangelicals" is a modern descriptor, but such is not the case. Webster's original 1828 dictionary defined "evangelical" as "consonant to the doctrines and precepts of the gospel published by Christ and His apostles; sound in the doctrines of the gospel; orthodox." Modern definitions have changed little, currently meaning "belonging to or designating the Christian churches that emphasize the teachings and authority of the Scriptures, especially of the New Testament . . . and that stress as paramount the tenet that salvation is achieved by personal conversion to faith in the atonement of Christ." [10] Therefore, whether using the old or the new definition, numbers of the Founding Fathers do indeed conform to the appellation "evangelical."

Similarly, few today know that of the fifty-six Founding Fathers who signed the Declaration in Independence Hall in 1776, over half had received degrees from schools that today would be considered seminaries or Bible  schools. [11] In fact, it was signers of the Declaration of Independence who started the Sunday School movement as well as several Bible societies and missionary societies. They were also responsible for penning numerous religious works and publishing many famous Bibles, including one by signer John Witherspoon in 1791, [12] another by Charles Thomson in 1808 [13] (Thomson and John Hancock were the only two individuals to sign the Declaration on July 4, 1776; on August 2, the others signed the famous copy so familiar today), and one by Dr. Benjamin Rush in 1812. [14] In fact, a famous 1782 Bible directly connected to Independence Hall is an important part of America's Godly heritage.

WITHERSPOON (LEFT) HAD A DIRECT HAND IN AMERICA'S FIRST FAMILY BIBLE (1791); THOMSON (MIDDLE) MADE THE FIRST AMERICAN TRANSLATION OF THE GREEK SEPTUAGINT (1808); AND RUSH (RIGHT) WAS RESPONSIBLE FOR AMERICA'S FIRST STEREOTYPED BIBLE (1812).

When Americans were still British citizens before the Revolution, it had been illegal to print English-language Bibles in America, but with the final American victory over the British at Yorktown, that policy was terminated. Robert Aitken, a local Philadelphia printer, therefore approached Congress, seeking permission to print an English-language Bible on his presses, pointing out that it would be "a neat edition of the Holy Scriptures for the use of schools." [15]

Congress agreed, approved his request, and appointed a congressional committee to oversee the project. [16] In late summer, 1782, the committee announced that the Bible was ready for print; [17] on September 12, 1782, Congress officially approved that Bible [18] and it soon began rolling off the presses – the first English-language Bible ever printed in America. In the front of that Bible is a congressional endorsement declaring:

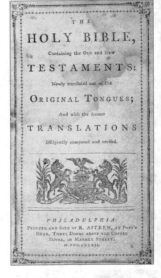

> Whereupon, *Resolved*, That the United States in Congress assembled . . . recommend this edition of the Bible to the inhabitants of the United States. [19]

Of this event – and the Bible it produced – an early historian observed:

> Who, in view of this fact, will call in question the assertion that this is a Bible nation? Who will charge the government with indifference to religion when the first Congress of the states assumed all the rights and performed all the duties of a Bible Society long before such an institution had an existence in the world! [20]

Another well-documented (but today unfamiliar) part of America's Godly heritage involves the account of a young George Washington during a fierce military battle in which his life precariously hung in the balance for two hours but was miraculously spared. In fact, fol-

A YOUNG WASHINGTON MIRACULOUSLY SPARED DURNG A PARTICULARLY FIERCE BATTLE

lowing that event, Washington himself openly acknowledged that it had been by the direct intervention of God that he remained alive.

The incident occurred during America's French and Indian War (1753-1763). At that time, England and France – two long-standing bitter enemies that had warred against each other for centuries in Europe – claimed the same land in America along the Ohio and Mississippi rivers. They went to war to settle that dispute; those living in America at the time took sides, with most of the Indians joining the French and most of the American colonists joining the British.

Great Britain, seeking to drive the French from the inland parts of America, dispatched 2,300 handpicked, veteran British troops to the colonies. Those troops, under the command of distinguished veteran General Edward Braddock, arrived in Virginia and were joined by a hundred Virginia buckskins, led by their twenty-three year old colonel, George Washington. They then set out for the mouth of the Ohio River to expel the French from Ft. Duquesne (now the city of Pittsburgh, Pennsylvania).

GEN. BRADDOCK

Having marched hundreds of miles, Braddock temporarily halted his troops at Fort Cumberland. They were still more than a hundred miles from the French fort, but Fort Cumberland would serve as a staging ground for the attack. Braddock dispatched his force in four waves, with himself, George Washington, the Virginians, and 1,200 chosen British troops comprising the third wave and principal military force (the first two groups had been the engineering force with its workers and their military protection, sent out to open a road

YOUNG COL. WASHINGTON

through the wilderness; the fourth group was the baggage and equipment wagons bringing up the rear). By July 9, 1755, Braddock's force had moved within seven miles of the French fort, and while following a path leading through a wooded ravine, they marched into a waiting ambush; the French and Indians opened fire on them from both sides.

Fortunately, Braddock's group was composed largely of battle-hardened British veterans accustomed to war, but unfortunately they

were veterans of European wars. European warfare was traditionally conducted in the open: one army lined up at one end of an open field and the other army lined up at the opposite end; they faced each other, took aim, and fired. The British now found themselves in the Pennsylvania woods with the French and Indians firing at them from the tops of trees, behind rocks, and under logs; the British were completely unfamiliar with woodland warfare.

When they came under fire, they responded according to their train-ing and lined up shoulder-to-shoulder along the bottom of the ravine; not surprisingly, they were promptly slaughtered. Over the next two hours, 714 of the 1,300 British and American troops were shot down, with only thirty of the French and Indians being shot – nearly all of those by Washington's Virginia buckskins, who were accustomed to woodland warfare and had sought cover when the attack began.

Even among the officers the British losses had been enormous: of the eighty-six British and American officers in that battle, twenty-six were killed and thirty-six more wounded. Significantly, George Washington was the <u>only</u> mounted officer not shot down off his horse – and he had been particularly vulnerable, having courageously ridden back and forth along the front lines, delivering General Braddock's orders among the troops.

Late in the battle General Braddock was seriously wounded and Washington took charge, gathering the remaining troops and heading back toward Fort Cumberland. Along the way, Braddock died, and on his death, Washington performed the role of a military chaplain, conducting the funeral service, reading Scriptures, and offering prayers. [21] Braddock's body was buried in the middle of the road, with

COL. WASHINGTON CONDUCTING GEN. BRADDOCK'S FUNERAL

wagons driving over his grave to prevent the Indians from finding and desecrating his remains.

Washington and the remaining troops arrived back at Fort Cumberland on July 17, 1755. During the week-long return to the fort, word had spread across the colonies that the slaughter of the British and Americans had been complete – that the entire force had been wiped out; so after his safe arrival at the fort, Washington wrote a letter to his family, assuring them that despite reports to the contrary, he was still very much alive:

> As I have heard since my arrival at this place a circumstantial account of my death and dying speech, I take this early opportunity of contradicting both and of assuring you that I now exist and appear in the land of the living. [22]

Having confirmed his safety to his family, he then recounted what had occurred during the battle – that when he had removed his jacket at the end of the battle, he found four bullet holes through it but not a single bullet had touched him; he had horses shot from under him, but he had not been scratched. He therefore concluded:

> I now exist and appear in the land of the living by the miraculous care of Providence that protected me beyond all human expectation. [23]

As word of God's Divine protection of Washington spread across the colonies, the Rev. Samuel Davies even referred to the incident in a sermon only a few weeks after the momentous battle. (Davies was a leader in the American revival known as the Great Awakening and was considered the greatest pulpit preacher in America.) Significantly, the devastating defeat of the British troops left American settlers on the frontier completely unprotected. They therefore banded together into volunteer military companies to defend their homes

THE REV. SAMUEL DAVIES

against impending French and Indian attack; the special sermon by the Rev. Davies was delivered to a group of these citizens just before they marched out. In that sermon, Davies told the brave volunteers:

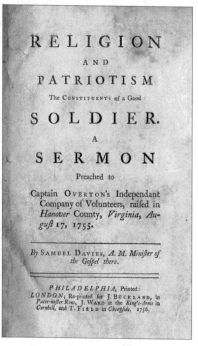

> He [God] that sent out Paul and his brethren to conquer the nations with the gentler weapons of plain truth, miracles, and the love of a crucified Savior, He – even that same Gracious Power – has formed and raised up . . . a William and a Marlborough [courageous military leaders in English history] and inspired them with this enterprising, intrepid [courageous] spirit . . . to save nations on the brink of ruin. . . . Our continent is like[ly] to become the seat of war, and we, for the future . . . have no other way left to defend our rights and privileges. And

has God been pleased to diffuse some sparks of this martial [military] fire through our country? I hope He has; and . . . may I not produce you – my brethren who are engaged in this expedition – as instances of it? As a remarkable instance of this, I may point out to the public that heroic youth Col. Washington, whom I cannot but hope Providence has hitherto preserved in so signal [remarkable] a manner for some important service to his country. [24]

Davies' expectant hope for the young Washington proved to be quite accurate. Twenty years later, it was apparent that God definitely had selected Washington for an "important service to his country," and the entire nation has benefited as a result. In fact, nearly two centuries later President Calvin Coolidge confirmed:

He [Washington] was the directing spirit without which there would have been no independence, no Union, no Constitution, and no Republic. . . . We cannot yet estimate him. We can only indicate our reverence for him and thank the Divine Providence which kept him to serve and inspire his fellow man. [25]

Significantly, Washington himself recognized that the critical role he had played in America's formation was not the result of his own skills but rather the favor of God. As he openly acknowledged, "I have only been an instrument in the hands of Providence." [26]

Additional evidence of just how miraculous had been Washington's preservation in 1755 was provided fifteen years later in 1770 when Washington had occasion to return to the same Pennsylvania woods where he had earlier battled the French and Indians. An old Indian chief, hearing that Washington had come back to that area, traveled to meet with him. The ancient leather-faced chief sat down with him over a council fire and announced that he had been a leader in the battle against Washington fifteen years earlier.

The chief recounted that during the battle, he had instructed his braves to single out the officers and shoot them down, knowing that if they could slaughter the officers, they could scatter the remaining troops and then easily destroy them later. Like the other officers, Washington had been specifically singled out. In fact, the chief proudly explained that his rifle had never before been known to miss, but after having personally fired at Washington seventeen different times without effect, he concluded that Washington was under the care of the Great Spirit and therefore instructed his braves to stop firing at him. He then told Washington:

I have traveled a long and weary path that I might see the young warrior of the great battle. [27] [I am] come to pay hom-

age to the man who is the particular favorite of Heaven, and
who [can] never die in battle. [28]

This remarkable account of God's direct intervention in the life of
one of our national heroes appeared in American history textbooks
for nearly a century and a half; it is a well-documented part of our
Godly heritage but is an account virtually unknown today. In fact, now
we are regularly told just the opposite – that America had no Godly
heritage and that our Founding Fathers were atheists, agnostics, and
deists who formed a completely secular government. However, a clear
pronouncement by Founding Father John Adams proves otherwise.
Adams forcefully declared:

> The general principles on which the fathers achieved inde-
> pendence were . . . the general principles of Christianity. [29]

Founding Fathers such as John Adams emphatically refute the
claims of today's secularists and revisionists.

Furthermore, abundant documentary evidence proves that the
general principles of Christianity were indeed firmly embraced by
the vast majority of our Founding Fathers, and that those principles
formed the foundation of American government. In fact, in addition
to the proof that is readily evident in the Founders' own writings and
public acts, additional confirmation is also found in what many today
might consider a surprising source: the publications of the American
Tract Society. That organization, noted for publishing Gospel tracts
and literature, was formed in the early 1800s; and significantly, several
of its published tracts were penned by famous Founding Fathers. [30]
Yet, considering the educational system and textbooks that produced
our great Founding Fathers, it is not surprising that so many were
Christians and were outspoken about the importance of Christian
principles in American government.

One early textbook of great influence was *The New England
Primer*. First introduced in Boston in 1690, it was a schoolbook from
which Americans learned to read until 1930; it is what would today

be described as a first grade textbook. Not only were many of the Founding Fathers raised on this textbook but they even reprinted it to make sure that it was available for children in their generation. (For example, Samuel Adams reprinted the *Primer* for students in Massachusetts, [31] Benjamin Franklin for students in Pennsylvania, [32] and Noah Webster for students in Connecticut. [33])

SAMUEL ADAMS (LEFT), BENJAMIN FRANKLIN (MIDDLE), AND NOAH WEBSTER (RIGHT)
EACH REPRINTED *THE NEW ENGLAND PRIMER* FOR STUDENTS IN THEIR STATES

After introducing students to the alphabet, the *Primer* presented a special section to be memorized – a section in which each letter of the alphabet was accompanied by a Bible verse:

A – A wise son makes a glad father, but a foolish son is the heaviness of his mother [Proverbs 10:1].

B – Better is little with the fear of the Lord than great treasure and trouble therewith [Proverbs 15:16].

C – Come unto Christ all ye that labor and are heavy laden and He will give you rest [Matthew 11:28].

In the back of this first grade book were over a hundred questions, including:

WHAT's right and good now shew me
Lord, and lead me by thy grace and
word. Thus shall I be a child of God, and
love and fear thy hand and rod.

An Alphabet of Lessons for Youth.

A Wise son maketh a glad father, but a foolish son is the heaviness of his mother.

B Etter is a little with the fear of the Lord, than great treasure & trouble therewith.

C Ome unto Christ all ye that labor and are heavy laden and he will give you rest.

D O not the abominable thing which I hate saith the Lord.

E Xcept a man be born again, he cannot see the kingdom of God.

F Oolishness is bound up in the heart of a child, but the rod of correction shall drive it far from him.

G ODLINESS is profitable unto all things, having the promise of the life that now is, and that which is to come.

H OLINESS becomes G O D's house for ever.

I T is good for me to draw near unto GOD.

Which is the fifth commandment?

What is forbidden in the fifth commandment?

What is required in the sixth commandment?

What is forbidden in the sixth commandment?

> Q. 63. *Which is the fifth commandment?*
> A. The fifth commandment is, *Honor thy father and thy mother, that thy days may be long upon the land which the Lord thy God giveth thee.*
> Q. 64. *What is required in the fifth commandment?*
> A. The fifth commandment requireth the preserving the honor, and performing the duties belonging to every one in their several places and relations, as superiors, inferiors, or equals.
> Q. 65. *What is forbidden in the fifth commandment?*
> A. The fifth commandment forbiddeth the neglecting of, or doing any thing against the honour and duty which belongeth to every one in their several places and relations.
> Q. 66. *What is the reason annexed to the fifth commandment?*

There were dozens of similar Bible-oriented questions.

Students educated under this system were frequently characterized by what many today would consider exceptional achievements at a very young age. For example, when John Quincy Adams was only eleven years old, he was assigned to be the official secretary to his father, John Adams, America's Ambassador to the British Court of Saint James; [34] and at the still tender age of fourteen, he was appointed as the official diplomatic secretary to Francis Dana, America's Ambassador to Russia. [35] (For many similar examples of achievement, see *Four Centuries of American Education*, available at www.wallbuilders.com.)

JOHN QUINCY ADAMS

John Quincy Adams' distinguished political career spanned seven decades. Following his service in the American Revolution, he was a foreign ambassador under Presidents George Washington, John Adams, and James Madison. In fact, Washington said that he was "the most valuable public character we have abroad, and will prove himself to be the ablest of all our Diplomatic Corps." [36] Adams was also a U. S. Senator under President Thomas Jefferson, Secretary of State under President James Monroe, and then was elected the nation's sixth President before finishing his career with an additional seventeen years in the U. S. House of Representatives.

On July 4, 1837 (sixty-one years after the Declaration had been signed), a very elderly John Quincy Adams delivered a patriotic oration to a large gathering in Massachusetts. Having been an eye-witness and a participant in the birth of America, he had been selected as the keynote speaker at the celebration. Adams began by asking the assembled crowd a rhetorical question – and then answering it:

JOHN QUINCY ADAMS

> Why is it that, next to the birthday of the Savior of the World, your most joyous and most venerated festival returns on this day [i.e., on the Fourth of July]? Is it not that in the chain of human events, the birthday of the nation is indissolubly linked with the birthday of the Savior? That it forms a leading event in the progress of the gospel dispensation? Is it not that the Declaration of Independence first organized the social compact on the foundation of the Redeemer's mission upon earth? That it laid the cornerstone of human government upon the first precepts of Christianity? [37]

According to John Quincy Adams, on the Fourth of July, 1776, the Founders had taken the principles that came into the world through the birth of Christ and used those principles to birth a nation, thus joining together Christian principles and civil government in an "indissoluble" bond.

Ironically, today's ivory tower elites assert just the opposite – they wrongly claim that the Founders did not want an indissoluble bond but rather that they wanted a so-called "separation" in order to keep Biblical principles out of civil government. Fortunately, however, the Founding Fathers' own records document their steadfast conviction that Christian principles were to be preserved in the civil arena. John Jay provides a clear example.

Jay was President of the Continental Congress during the Revolution and was one of the three Founding Fathers who drafted and signed the peace treaty with Great Britain to establish America as an independent nation. After the U. S. Constitution was written, Jay helped pen the *Federalist Papers* and is considered one of the three men most responsible for the adoption of the Constitution. When George Washington became President, Jay served first as his Secretary of State and then was appointed as the original Chief Justice of the U. S. Supreme Court.

Chief Justice John Jay, believing that Christian principles should be included in civil arenas, forcefully declared:

> Providence has given to our people the choice of their rulers; and it is the *duty* – as well as the privilege and interest – of our Christian nation to select and prefer Christians for their rulers. [38] (emphasis added)

President George Washington similarly urged the incorporation of religious principles throughout the public arena. In his famous "Farewell Address" in which he announced to Congress and the nation that he would retire from public office at the end of his second term, he offered candid advice on what it would take to keep America strong. For generations afterwards, Washington's Farewell Address was considered so important and its content so profound that it appeared as a separate, stand-alone school textbook; students were taught that this Address was the most significant political speech ever delivered to the nation and were tested on its content. Regrettably, however, Washington's Farewell Address has now largely disappeared from current textbooks – apparently because it has too much religious content for today's often secular-minded educrats.

As an example, secularists today ignore and even attempt to suppress Washington's unequivocal declaration in that Address as to what made the American political system so successful:

> Of all the dispositions and habits which lead to political prosperity, religion and morality are indispensable supports. In vain would that man claim the tribute of patriotism, who should labor to subvert these great pillars. [39]

Washington specifically identified religion and morality as the two most important elements of the American political system and even warned that anyone who attempted to separate those two elements from the political realm could not be considered an American patriot. Such anti-secular sentiments were expressed not only by Washington (as well as by Jay and Adams above) but also by numerous other Founding Fathers. [40]

America's system of government was deliberately and intentionally built upon religion and morality; it has subsequently enjoyed unprecedented success. America is now the world's longest on-going constitutional republic, and to exist more than two centuries under the same governing document is an accomplishment unknown among contemporary nations. For example, during the same time that America has had just one government, France has had fifteen; [41] and in just the twentieth century alone, Russia had four; [42] Afghanistan, five; [43] Poland, seven; [44] etc.

Significantly, each nation had access to the same body of political philosophies and writings when forming their governments; yet our Founding Fathers evidently selected ideas that the other nations chose not to apply. What were the sources of the Founders' successful ideas?

Political science professors believed that this question could be answered by examining a broad spectrum of writings from the Founding Era with the goal of identifying the sources cited in those writings. The researchers assembled 15,000 representative writings from that period and isolated 3,154 direct quotes in those writings. At the end of ten years, they had traced the quotes back to their original sources, thereby identifying the most frequently-cited sources of the Founding Era. (The results of that study may be found in the book *The Origins of American Constitutionalism.* [45])

The individual who was cited most often in the writings of the Founding Era was political philosopher Charles Montesquieu, with 8.3 percent of the quotes being taken from his writings. [46] Legal scholar William Blackstone was next, with 7.9 percent of the quotes; [47] and political philosopher and theologian John Locke was third, with 2.9 percent. [48] These were the three most frequently-cited <u>individuals</u>

MONTESQUIEU (LEFT), BLACKSTONE (MIDDLE), AND LOCKE (RIGHT)

during the Founding Era, but the single most-cited <u>source</u> was the Bible, with 34 percent of the quotes coming from the Scriptures. [49]

Significantly, that percentage is even higher when the source of the ideas used by individuals such as Montesquieu, Blackstone, and Locke are identified and included. Consider, for example, a primary source of Blackstone's ideas.

Blackstone's most famous work was his *Commentaries on the Laws*. First introduced in 1766, it became the final word in American courts and remained a primary legal authority until well into the twentieth century: it was quoted to define words, establish procedure, and settle disputes. A primary source of Blackstone's ideas is evident even through a superficial examination of his writings, but the testimony of Charles Finney (1792-1875) also provides a clear confirmation.

Finney, a university president, educator, and civil rights leader, was probably best known as a famous revivalist during America's Second Great Awakening of the early 1800s. In his autobiography, Finney recounted his early desire to become an attorney, so like all other law students at that time, he commenced a study of Blackstone's *Commentaries*. As Blackstone covered the various legal concepts, he frequently presented the Biblical ideas on which the laws were based. Finney stated that in the process of studying Blackstone, he read so much of the Bible that he became a Christian and received his call to the ministry. [50]

Clearly, then, a primary source of Blackstone's ideas was the Bible; and a survey of the writings of Montesquieu and Locke confirms a similar (and sometime even stronger) Biblical influence on their writings. Therefore, while thirty-four percent of the quotes in the representative writings of the Founding Era came directly from the Bible, many of the other quotes were taken from writers who, like Blackstone, had used the Bible to help arrive at their own conclusions. The Bible therefore was far and away the most influential source of ideas in the Founding Era.

Consequently, it is not surprising that the Constitution reflects many Biblical principles. For example, Isaiah 33:22 sets forth three distinct branches of government; the logic for the separation of powers was based on teachings derived from Jeremiah 17:9; the basis of tax exemptions for churches (exemptions originated by the Founding Fathers [51]) can be found in Ezra 7:24; and there are many other examples of American government applying Biblical patterns and precedents.

The Biblical underpinnings of America were so obvious to previous generations that in 1892, even the U. S. Supreme Court had no difficulty in rendering a unanimous decision declaring:

> [N]o purpose of action against religion can be imputed to any legislation, state or national, because this is a religious people. . . . [T]his is a Christian nation. [52]

What would lead the U. S. Supreme Court to conclude that America was a Christian nation? The simple answer is, America's own history.

The Court's decision was only sixteen pages long, but even in that short span, the Court provided almost eighty different historical precedents. The Court cited statements of the Founding Fathers, acts of Congress and state governments, and numerous others official documents, even noting that there were many additional volumes of historical precedents also proving that America was a Christian nation. Eighty precedents in a case is not only impressive but it is also important, for courts seek to base their decisions on precedent; this enables them to be consistent from ruling to ruling, thus contributing to a stable society.

Significantly, that 1892 Court decision was by no means the only Supreme Court decision that recognized and preserved America's Biblical heritage; similar decisions were rendered both before and after that ruling. For example, in 1844, a school run by the city of Philadelphia adopted a policy prohibiting Christian ministers from setting foot on campus. That school, originally founded by a wealthy French immigrant, was operated on the philosophy dominant in France during the French Enlightenment (and embraced by many public schools today) that students could successfully learn morality apart from Christianity or the Bible.

This policy, perceived as an attempt to keep the Bible from students, became an issue at the U. S. Supreme Court. The Court's ruling on that subject was unanimous and was delivered by Justice Joseph Story, called a "Father of American Jurisprudence" and placed on the Court by President James Madison. In that decision, the Court declared:

Why may not the Bible, and especially the New Testament . . . be read and taught as a divine revelation in the [school] – its general precepts expounded . . . and its glorious principles of morality inculcated? . . . Where can the purest principles of morality be learned so clearly or so perfectly as from the New Testament? [53]

The Supreme Court of the United States unanimously held that this government-run school should teach Christianity and the Bible, the source of "the purest principles of morality." Modern rulings are exactly opposite, but few today realize that earlier Courts – Courts whose Justices were appointed by Founding Fathers – have already addressed the same issues.

There are literally dozens of such rulings, including one by the 1811 New York Supreme Court – a ruling subsequently cited by the U. S.

Supreme Court as an authority for its own decisions. That New York case dealt with a man who had distributed a writing full of vulgar, malicious, and gratuitous profanity attacking God, Jesus Christ, and the Bible. He was fined and punished, and on appeal the state supreme court upheld the conviction, stressing that:

> [W]hatever strikes at the root of Christianity tends manifestly to the dissolution of civil government. [54]

According to this court, an attack on Christianity was an attack on the foundation of the country and its government – and the U. S. Supreme Court agreed. [55] Significantly, none of these court decisions was a problem with the First Amendment, because previous generations understood that the First Amendment was not to be used to secularize the public square.

While Americans today are accustomed to hearing the First Amendment coupled with the phrase "separation of church and state," the religious clauses of the First Amendment only state:

> Congress shall make no law respecting an establishment of religion or prohibiting the free exercise thereof.

Clearly, neither the word "separation," "church," nor "state" is found in any part of the First Amendment. In fact, that phrase appears in no governmental founding document. Most recognize the phrase, but few know its source; yet it is important to understand the origins of that phrase and its subsequent coupling with the First Amendment.

Significantly, the ninety Founding Fathers who framed the First Amendment articulated a very clear intent. The debates surrounding the framing of the First Amendment spanned from June 7 through September 25 of 1789, and the records of those

debates make unequivocally clear that the First Amendment's purpose was to limit the federal government in two specific areas.

First, the federal government was prohibited from establishing a national denomination, whether Catholic, Anglican, or any other. This problem had plagued America when she had been part of Great Britain: the British government could decree an official denomination to which all citizens must belong and then punish those who refused. The Founders sought to prevent that evil through what is now termed the First Amendment's Establishment Clause ("Congress shall make no law respecting an <u>establishment</u> of religion . . . ").

Secondly, the First Amendment barred the federal government from interfering with or limiting the people's public religious expressions. This part of the First Amendment is called the Free Exercise Clause (" . . . or prohibiting the <u>free exercise</u> thereof"). This clause required the federal government to protect (rather than suppress, as it currently does) public religious expressions. Because of the Free Exercise Clause, the federal government could not prohibit the people's free exercise of religion, whether expressed in private or public.

Significantly, both religion clauses of the First Amendment were to limit the federal government, **_not_** the people – that is, first, the _government_ could not establish any national religious conformity, and second, the _government_ could not stop public religious expressions but must protect them.

This is the extent of the First Amendment's religion clauses; and not only does the phrase "separation of church and state" not appear in any part of that Amendment but significantly, according to the official records, not one Framer ever mentioned that phrase throughout any of the official discussions on the First Amendment. (It does seem that if "separation of church and state" had been their great intent for the First Amendment, one of its ninety Framers would have said something about it; none did.) Significantly, the phrase appeared in a private letter penned by President Thomas Jefferson some thirteen years _after_ the First Amendment was written.

Throughout his life, Jefferson had prov-
en himself to be a firm friend of religious
liberty. In fact, before the Revolution in
his own state of Virginia, he had fought
for freedom of public religious expression
for Baptists, Quakers, Presbyterians, and
others who were not part of the British
state-established Anglican Church. [56]
(Significantly, in various colonies prior to
the Revolution, non-Anglican ministers had

actually been severely persecuted and even put to death for preaching
the Gospel without the permission of the state-established church. [57])
Jefferson (and Patrick Henry, James Madison, George Washington,
George Mason, and others [58]) fought for the rights of religious expression for all Christians, including the Baptists, and had done so not only
before America separated from Great Britain but afterwards as well.

Consequently, the Baptists were elated when in 1801 Jefferson became the nation's third President, for a leader who had proven himself
their champion at the state level was now the national leader. Among
the favorable correspondence he received from Baptists across the
country [59] was one from the Baptists of Danbury, Connecticut, who
wrote a letter congratulating him on his victory, celebrating his election
as president, and offering their prayers for him; but they also expressed
their concern that the government might restrict their public religious
expressions. They asserted that freedom of religion was a God-given
inalienable right and that the government was to be powerless to restrict religious activities unless, as they explained, those activities caused
someone to "work ill to his neighbor" [60] – that is, unless someone's
religious expression actually directly injured someone else.

Jefferson understood their concern, for he had already proven that
it was his own. He therefore wrote the Danbury Baptists on January 1, 1802, thanking them for their "kind prayers." He then assured
them that their free exercise of religion was indeed an inalienable

right and would <u>not</u> be meddled with by the government because there was a "wall of separation between church and state" that would prevent the government from interfering with or hindering religious activities. [61]

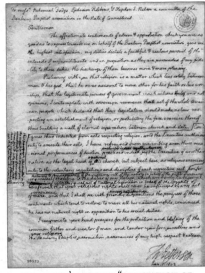

Jefferson, like the other Founders, fully understood that the First Amendment was to protect rather than prevent public religious expressions and that this is what "separation of church and state" secured. For a century-and-a-half after Jefferson's letter, there was no misunderstanding about either the purpose of the First Amendment or the meaning of Jefferson's phrase.

For example, in 1853 (half-a-century after Jefferson had written that phrase) a group petitioned Congress, urging them to separate Christian principles from government, with chaplains being turned out of Congress and the military, and Christian principles being removed from government and the official public square. They desired a

so-called "separation of church and state," but in the wrong direction – that is, instead of the government protecting religious expressions in the public arena, they wanted the government to remove them. Congress examined that possibility and then emphatically rejected it, declaring:

Had the people during the Revolution had a suspicion of any attempt to war against Christianity, that Revolution would have been strangled in its cradle. At the time of the adoption of the Constitution and the amendments, the universal sentiment was that Christianity should be encouraged, [but] not any one [denomination]. . . . In this age, there is no substitute for Christianity. . . . That was the religion of the founders of the republic and they expected it to remain the religion of their descendants. [62]

In short, Congress affirmed that the First Amendment (and consequently its so-called "separation of church and state") had never been intended to secularize the public square but just the opposite. In fact, two years later, Congress reiterated:

[T]he great, vital, and conservative element in our system is the belief of our people in the pure doctrines and divine truths of the Gospel of Jesus Christ. [63]

Not only Congress but also the Supreme Court refused to separate Christian principles from the public arena. For example, in an 1878 case (more than three-quarters of a century after Jefferson had penned his "separation" letter), the plaintiffs invoked Jefferson's phrase, hoping to use it to their advantage. Significantly, the Supreme Court responded not by merely citing Jefferson's metaphor (which is all that most courts today do) but rather by reprinting a lengthy segment from his letter to prove that "separation of church and state" was to preserve rather than remove Christian values and practices in public policy. [64]

The courts maintained that position until 1947 when a radical change occurred. In *Everson v. Board of Education* the Court cited only Jefferson's "separation" metaphor, ignoring the rest of his letter and its clear context. It therefore boldly announced a new standard:

The First Amendment has erected a wall between church and state. That wall must be kept high and impregnable. We could not approve the slightest breach. [65]

Under this new philosophy, no longer would Jefferson's separation phrase protect public religious expressions as it had for a century-and-a-half, it would now become a mandate to exclude them and to secularize the public square.

Significantly, as courts and secularists began to expunge public religious expressions, they simultaneously clamored "separation of church and state," asserting "This is what the Founders wanted – this is their great intent!" So often have they repeated the separation metaphor when talking about the First Amendment that many now believe that the phrase is actually part of the Amendment, thus demonstrating the truth of a statement attributed to Dr. William James (the "Father of Modern Psychology"):

> There is nothing so absurd but if you repeat it often enough people will believe it. [66]

In fact, contemporary courts, in dealing with First Amendment issues, now repeat the separation phrase more often than they do the Constitution itself. (Since 1947, the separation phrase has been cited in over four thousand cases but the First Amendment has been cited in less than three thousand. [67]) The courts have now elevated a single phrase from a private letter – a phrase completely reversed from its original meaning – above the actual language of the First Amendment itself.

Having announced its new approach in 1947, in 1962 the Supreme Court first nationally implemented the agenda of public secularism when – for the first time in American history – it ordered the separation of religious principles from education, ruling that thenceforward it would be unconstitutional for a student even <u>voluntarily</u> to pray at school. [68] (Significantly, secularists and legal revisionists today wrongly assert that the Court decision in that case was only protecting stu-

dents who were being forced to pray, but the Court itself clearly disputes that assertion, openly acknowledging that the unconstitutional prayer had been completely voluntary. [69])

Following that initial decision, the courts steadily expanded outward their hostility toward voluntary student prayer. For example, while a 1965 court permitted prayers if they were silent, [70] by 1985, the Supreme Court had ruled that even <u>silent</u> prayer was unconstitutional. [71] (Interestingly, how can the Court be sure when silent prayers are occurring? After all, many occur with heads unbowed and eyes open, so how does the Court know when to enforce its ban on silent prayer?)

The landmark 1962 case not only reversed the Constitution's protection for religious expressions by misrepresenting the separation phrase but it also redefined the meaning of the word "church" within the misused metaphor. For the previous two centuries, the word "church" in the phrase "separation of church and state" had been defined to mean a federally-established national denomination such as was represented by the Baptists, Catholics, Anglicans, Presbyterians, etc., [72] but in 1962 the Court determined that "church" would now mean a religious <u>activity</u> instead of a religious <u>institution</u>. As a result, the First Amendment no longer simply prevented the federal government from setting up a national denomination (which voluntary prayer certainly did not do), but it now meant that the federal government must not <u>allow</u> a public religious activity (which voluntary prayer certainly was). This was the turning point in the modern interpretation of the First Amendment; and since that time, every possible genre of traditional public religious expression has been forbidden under the new doctrine.

However, the 1962 case was notable not only for its redefinition of the First Amendment but also for its lack of precedent. Recall that when the 1892 Supreme Court unanimously ruled that Christian

principles must remain the basis of American laws and institutions
it had offered nearly eighty precedents; but the 1962 case had been
quite the contrary, providing virtually no precedents to support its
removal of voluntary school prayer. [73] The Justices were simply ready
to move America in a new direction, so in essence they simply announced: "We will not permit voluntary prayers in schools anymore
we now think that such expressions violate the Constitution." Within
twelve months of that original decision, in two additional cases the
Court reaffirmed its removal of voluntary prayer and broadened its
prohibition to include Bible reading at school. [74]

The ban on Bible reading was an even
more radical reversal than the removal
of voluntary prayer. Recall from the brief
historical survey already presented that
the Founders relied on the Bible in education, early textbooks inculcated the Bible
and used it to help students memorize the
alphabet, Congress printed the first English-language Bible for the use of schools,
and previous Supreme Courts ruled that
government-run schools would teach the Bible. So how did the Court
justify its 1963 ban on Bible reading in public schools?

One need only read the written opinion in that case (available either
online or at any local county law library) to answer this question. In
reaching its decision, the lower court had relied on the testimony
of a psychologist who explained the danger of reading the Bible in
schools, and the Supreme Court then repeated that testimony in its
decision, reporting:

> [I]f portions of the New Testament were read without explana-
> tion, they could be and . . . had been psychologically harmful
> to the child. [75]

Amazingly, the Court was no longer concerned merely about law
and the Constitution (its constitutionally assigned role), but it had

now appointed itself as the national child psychologist. In fact, in recent years, Justices on the Court have described its role not only as being amateur psychologists on a "psycho-journey" [76] but also as being "a national theology board" [77] and "a super board of education for every school district in the nation." [78]

Significantly, the decision to remove the Bible from schools, just like the decision to ban voluntary prayer, was a reversal of all previous practice and rulings by the Court on that issue. The 1963 Court was simply announcing yet another new position, in essence saying, "The majority of the nine of us on the Court simply don't want the Bible in schools any more!"

Following those two landmark rulings, courts continued to expand their new secular mandates outward. For example, in 1967, a federal court declared a four line nursery rhyme used by a K-5 kindergarten class to be unconstitutional. The court acknowledged that the word "God" did not appear anywhere in the nursery rhyme; nevertheless, it was still unconstitutional. [79] Apparently, if someone were to hear the rhyme, he might *think* that it was talking about God, and that would be unconstitutional. This trend of hostility toward religious expressions continued in case after case, year after year.

In fact, by 1980, the Supreme Court even addressed whether students could continue <u>voluntarily</u> to see the Ten Commandments while at school. The Ten Commandments in question were acknowledged to be passive displays, just one of many pictures at school. That is, a student might see hanging on the wall of the school a picture of George Washington, or a field of flowers, or the Ten Commandments, or a lighthouse on a seashore, or student artwork, etc. The Ten Commandments were not part of any curriculum; they passively hung on the wall, and like any other picture, a student could look at them if he wanted to, and if he didn't, he just walked on by.

Honor thy father
and thy mother

Thou shalt not
kill

Thou shalt not
commit adultery

Thou shalt not
steal

Thou shalt not
bear false witness

Thou shalt not
covet

Nevertheless, the Supreme Court ruled that allowing students even voluntarily to see a passive copy of the Ten Commandments at school was unconstitutional. As the Court explained:

> If the posted copies of the Ten Commandments are to have any effect at all, it will be to induce the schoolchildren to read, meditate upon, perhaps to venerate and obey the Commandments. . . . [This] is not a permissible state objective. [80]

What amazing logic! – students can't see the Ten Commandments even if they want to, for they might obey "religious" teachings such as "don't steal" and "don't kill," and that would be unconstitutional!

Yet generations of American leaders and legal authorities prior to that ruling had consistently and frequently affirmed that the Ten Commandments were the basis of civilized behavior in society and a foundation of our legal code. As John Adams asserted:

> If "Thou shalt not covet," and "Thou shalt not steal," were not commandments of Heaven, they must be made inviolable precepts in every society before it can be civilized or made free. [81]

Significantly, John Adams is an authority on the First Amendment. He oversaw its framing in the U. S. Senate and his signature is one of only two that appears at the bottom of that document; and he forcefully asserts that the Ten Commandments must be the fundamental precepts of our civil society.

James Wilson also affirmed the importance of Divine laws such as the Ten Commandments. Wilson signed both the Declaration of Independence and the Constitution, was appointed by President George Washington as an original Justice on the U. S. Supreme Court, and founded the first organized legal training in America. [82] He certainly is qualified to speak to what is constitutional; and concerning the role of Divine laws such as the Ten Commandments, he forcefully declared:

> Human law <u>must</u> rest its authority ultimately upon the authority of that law which is Divine. . . . Far from being rivals or enemies, religion and law are twin sisters, friends, and mutual assistants. [83] (emphasis added)

James Wilson certainly did not believe that the Ten Commandments should be kept from public view, and many other Founders made similarly explicit comments about the importance of Divine law and the Ten Commandments. [84] Additionally, earlier courts issued literally dozens of rulings citing from the Ten Commandments as a legal authority on numbers of diverse issues. [85] In fact, so clear was the civil recognition of America's reliance on the Decalogue that for decades one was more likely to find a copy of the Ten Commandments hanging in a government building than a religious one! Yet despite this lengthy history of legal reliance on the Ten Commandments, the Court suddenly held that students could no longer see the teachings that are the basis of our laws.

Returning to the landmark 1962 case that initiated the official hostility toward public religious expressions, the entire controversy had begun with a twenty-two word voluntary prayer that the Court struck down in the *Engel v. Vitale* case. The little prayer that led to the end of all school prayer and other public religious expressions had simply stated:

> Almighty God, we acknowledge our dependence upon Thee and we beg Thy blessings upon us, our parents, our teachers and our country. [86]

That voluntary prayer was so bland that eight years later it was described by a court as a "To-Whom-It-May-Concern" prayer. [87] That simple prayer acknowledged God only once – the same number of times that God is acknowledged in the Pledge of Allegiance, and only one-fourth the number of times in the Declaration of Independence. Nevertheless, that single voluntary acknowledgment was ruled unconstitutional.

But since this prayer had merely acknowledged God, the Court went so far as to investigate what percentage of the nation at that time did believe in God; it reported that only three percent of Americans professed no belief in religion [88] – i.e., no belief in God. Significantly, ninety-seven percent did believe – the twenty-two word prayer was therefore consistent with the beliefs of nearly all the nation, yet the Court ruled it unconstitutional for students even voluntarily to say what almost the entire nation believed. Prior to this decision, three percent had always been a minority, but this decision initiated the current policy whereby the philosophy of the small dissident group (i.e., the three percent) becomes the standard by which the rest of the nation (i.e., the ninety-seven percent) must conduct its public affairs.

Notice that in the unconstitutional twenty-two word prayer, there had been four categories over which God's blessings had been petitioned: (1) "us" – students, (2) "parents" – families, (3) "teachers" – schools, and (4) "the country" – the nation. Significantly, for almost two centuries the courts had applied Biblical principles in interpreting policy in each of those areas.

For example, in the area of families, even twentieth-century courts affirmed:

> Marriage was not originated by human law. When God created Eve, she was a wife to Adam; they then and there occupied the status of husband to wife and wife to husband. . . . The truth is that civil government has grown out of marriage . . . which created homes, and population, and society, from which government became necessary. . . . [Marriages] will produce a home and family that will contribute to good society, to free and just government,

and to the support of Christianity. . . . It would be sacrilegious to apply the designation "a civil contract" to such a marriage. It is that and more – a status ordained by God. [89]

The courts recognized that God (not government) had made marriage and the family, and that government therefore didn't have a right to regulate something it hadn't made. Courts further noted that civil laws made divorce difficult to obtain because the Bible made divorce difficult to obtain. As one court explained:

> This engagement [the legal contract of marriage] is the most solemn and important of human transactions. It is regarded by all Christian nations as the basis of civilized society. . . . The parties cannot dissolve the contract, as they can others, by mutual consent; and no light or trivial causes should be suffered to effect its rescission. . . . [T]he happiness of married life greatly depends on its indissolubility. [90]

Very simply, the courts regularly acknowledged and incorporated God's standards in policies on families; [91] and until 1962-63, they similarly applied Biblical principles to the other three categories as well. Did the decision to expunge God's principles from dealings in these areas have any measurable effect? Statistical measurements seem to indicate that it did – and in ways that the Founders themselves had predicted.

Consider, for example, the changes that occurred in the first category ("us" – students). George Washington in his "Farewell Address" had specifically warned:

> [L]et us with caution indulge the supposition that morality can be maintained without religion. Whatever may be conceded to the influence of refined education on minds of peculiar structure [that is, on the impressionable minds of students], reason and experience both forbid us to expect that national morality can prevail in exclusion of religious principle. [92]

Washington forewarned that excluding religious principles from education and students would result in a loss of morality; statistics affirm the accuracy of his warning.

For example, following the Court's exclusion of Biblical principles from students in 1962-63, birth rates for unmarried teens skyrocketed, [93] and birth rates for junior-high girls ages 10-14 soared nearly 460 percent. [94] Not only does America now have the highest teen-pregnancy rate of any nation in the industrialized world [95] but sexually-transmitted diseases among students reached previously unrecorded highs. [96] Clearly, moral measurements for "us" (i.e., students) broke violently in the wrong direction following the Court's 1962-63 decisions. The correlation is strong, and perhaps it is merely coincidental; nevertheless, it is clear and striking.

As already noted, public policy in the category of "our parents" (i.e., our families) long maintained the use of Biblical principles. Yet when Biblical principles were excluded from that area, the divorce rate suddenly skyrocketed [97] and

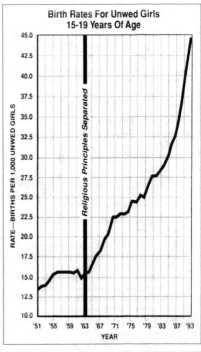

Birth Rates For Unwed Girls 15-19 Years Of Age

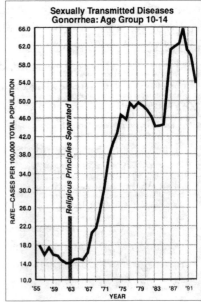

Sexually Transmitted Diseases Gonorrhea: Age Group 10-14

the United States found itself number one in the world in divorce. [98] Similarly, the number of single parent families also exploded, reaching almost triple its previous level, [99] and unmarried couples living together soared by over 1,000 percent. [100] In fact, having excluded Biblical principles, some American policymakers even became confused about how to define something as simple as marriage: was it to remain the union of a man and a woman, or should it become that of a man and a man, or five women and a man, or any of the other possible combinations? What remarkable changes have occurred since the Court excluded Biblical values from its public policies on the family!

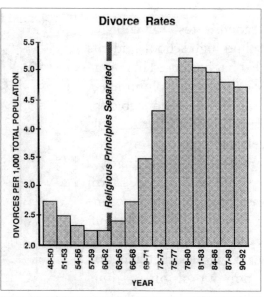

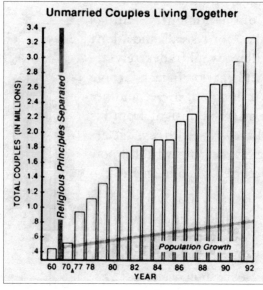

The third category over which God's assistance had been petitioned was "our teachers" (i.e., schools). What happened when God and Biblical principles were barred from schools? Interestingly, the

Scholastic Aptitude Test (an academic test for college-bound high school students that has been used in America since 1926) plummeted, after having been stable for decades. [101] Other school-related statistics showed similarly adverse changes.

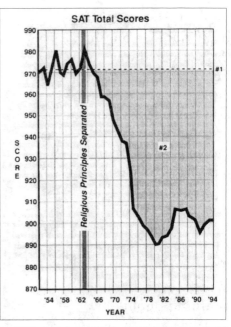

Consider finally the fourth category – that of "our country," or, the nation. Just from a common sense perspective, logic suggests that adopting a policy prohibiting individuals from seeing the Ten Commandments – things like "don't steal" and "don't kill" – would adversely affect behavior. In fact, George Washington, in yet another remarkable insight from his "Farewell Address," accurately predicted what has now occurred when he queried:

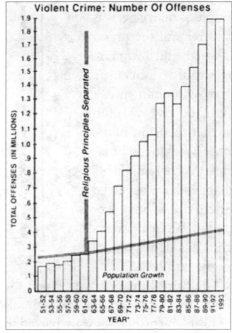

> Let it simply be asked, Where is the security for property, for reputation, for life, if the sense of religious obligation desert . . .? [102]

Washington understood that if the sense of religious obligation were separated from the public arena, there would be no security for life or property – the very things most often touched by violent crime. Significantly, following the Court's exclusion of Biblical principles, violent crime soared over 470 percent [103] and the United States became the world's leader in total crimes committed. [104] (There are many additional examples of marked change in national statistical measurements following 1962-63.)

The Founders understood that America could prosper only under God's blessings and therefore refused to separate His principles from any aspect of public affairs. As Benjamin Franklin confirmed:

> [W]ithout His concurring aid . . . we ourselves shall become a reproach and a byword down to future ages. [105]

The Founders recognized that for God to bestow His blessings, His principles had to be honored and embraced. As George Washington pointed out:

> [T]he propitious smiles of Heaven can never be expected on a nation that disregards the eternal rules of order and right which Heaven itself has ordained. [106]

In fact, the thought of disregarding what Washington identified as God's "eternal rules of order and right" was a fearful thought for the Founding Fathers. As Thomas Jefferson acknowledged:

> I tremble for my country when I reflect that God is just – that His justice cannot sleep forever. [107]

Of course, the Founders' reasoning that God would bless or oppose a nation based on the degree to which it embraced His policies makes sense only *if* there is a God, only *if* He has established transcendent rights and wrongs, and only *if* He responds to a nation on that basis. (However, if these "ifs" are true, then it offers a plausible explanation for the statistical correlation so apparent on the charts.)

Significantly, the Founders believed that these "ifs" <u>were</u> true, and they therefore repeatedly stressed that God should be openly and publicly acknowledged throughout the civic arena. For example, George Washington forcefully asserted:

> [I]t is the <u>duty</u> of all <u>nations</u> to <u>acknowledge</u> the providence of Almighty God, to obey His will, to be grateful for His benefits, and humbly to implore His protection and favor. [108] (emphasis added)

Samuel Adams similarly admonished:

> May every citizen . . . in the country have a proper sense of the Deity upon his mind and an impression of the declaration recorded in the Bible: "Him that honoreth Me, I will honor; but he that despiseth Me shall be lightly esteemed" [I Samuel 2:30]. [109]

Significantly, prior to 1962-63, America guided its public policy with clear cognizance of these principles, fully embracing the belief that when America honored God, God could bless America, but that if America adopted public policies that despised God and His standards, His blessings should no longer be expected. This belief stemmed from the principle of national accountability to God.

While this concept is not completely unknown today, it is the concept of individual accountability to God that is still widely accepted – most believe that someday they <u>will</u> stand before God and answer to Him for their behavior. Significantly, however, the Founders stressed both individual <u>and</u> national accountability, and they also understood a fundamental distinction between the two that is largely unacknowledged today: the difference of <u>*when*</u> that accountability would occur. They recognized that individuals would answer to God in the future but that nations would not – that when a nation died, it was forever dead and would not be resurrected in the future to answer for what it had done. So when does a nation answer to God?

As explained on the floor of the Constitutional Convention in 1787 by George Mason ("The Father of the Bill of Rights"):

> As nations cannot be rewarded or punished in the next world, they must be in this. By an inevitable chain of causes and effects, Providence punishes national sins by national calamities. [110]

Other Founders echoed the same truth: they believed that God would deal with a nation in the present for the stands it takes and the policies it enacts. [111]

Understanding the profound consequences of national accountability, the Founders were emphatic about keeping in office those who would enact policies that God could bless, for God's principles are incorporated into public policies only to the degree that those principles are embraced by the officials enacting the policies. Yet leaders who honor God's principles are placed into office only when voters themselves first embrace those principles and apply them as the standard to guide their vote. In short, if God-fearing citizens are not involved at the ballot box, God-fearing leaders will not be elected, God-honoring policies will not be enacted, and the respective city, state, or nation will not be blessed by God. Understanding this, Chief Justice John Jay reminded voters in his day:

> Providence has given to our people the choice of their rulers; and it is the <u>duty</u> – as well as the privilege and interest – of our Christian nation to select and prefer Christians for their rulers. [112] (emphasis added)

The Rev. Charles Finney (1792-1875) similarly reminded Christian voters in his day:

> [T]he time has come that Christians must vote for honest men and take consistent ground in politics. . . . Christians have been exceedingly guilty in this matter. But the time has come when they must act differently. . . . God cannot sustain this free and blessed country which we love and pray for unless the Church will take right ground. . . . He will bless or curse this nation according to the course [Christians] take [in politics]. [113]

News reporting today rarely mentions whether a candidate running for office embraces or rejects God-fearing values and Biblical principles; and many God-fearing citizens often complain that they don't know what a candidate really believes. Fortunately, a number of voter websites are now available to help identify the specific beliefs of candidates on numbers of important issues, including those related to Biblical values (links to several such websites are available at www.wallbuilders.com). Additionally, when a state or federal incumbent is running for reelection, numerous websites will present his voting record, thus clearly establishing what he has actually done while in office. (A voting record is always to be believed above a candidate's speeches or campaign ads, for as the old axiom correctly states, "Actions speak louder than words.")

God-fearing citizens <u>must</u> become active voters; they must also realize that "separation of church and state" as it exists today is not a teaching of the Founding Fathers, it is not an historical teaching, and it is not a teaching of law until recent years. While a separation between the two institutions of Church and State <u>is</u> to be strongly supported and vigorously pursued, that does <u>not</u> mean a separation of values, principles, and religious expressions from the public square. Furthermore, because of contemporary court rulings, the modern reality is that there _is_ going to be _someone's_ religion in the schools and the government.

For generations, the understanding of what constituted a "religion" was simple and straightforward: "religion" was defined as "a belief in the being and perfections of God, in the revelation of His will to man, in man's obligation to obey His commands, in a state of reward and punishment, and in man's accountableness to God." [114] Therefore, to be a religion required a belief in some Supreme Being who set forth commands by which he expected his followers to live and conduct their affairs – religion required a belief in the existence of some Supreme Being who was to be worshipped and obeyed by his followers. Consequently, from both a legal and historical standpoint, "religion comprehends the belief and worship of pagans and Mohammedans as well as of Christians; any religion consisting in the belief of a superior power or powers governing the world, and in the worship of such power or powers. Thus we speak of the religion of the Turks, of the Hindoos, of the Indians, &c. as well as of the Christian religion." [115] Significantly, groups that did not acknowledge some type of Supreme Being were <u>never</u> considered to be religions.

However, in the early 1960s when the Court decided to reject the long-standing meaning of the First Amendment, it also decided to reject the long-standing meaning of "religion"; and just as it wrote its own new First Amendment, it also wrote its own new definition for "religion" whereby whatever a person believed so strongly that it affected the way he behaved was considered his religion. [116] As a consequence, many beliefs, creeds, and philosophies that completely denied the existence of <u>any</u> Supreme Being suddenly became religions.

For example, courts now hold that atheism is a religion. [117] But since atheism is the essence of <u>anti</u>-religion, how can anti-religion be a religion? – what are the religious beliefs of atheists? Atheists devoutly believe that there should be <u>no</u> public religious expressions, so the religion of atheism is the religion of practicing no religious practice – that is, it is religiously practicing non-religion; and the courts officially consider it to be a First Amendment religion entitled to full *religious* protections.

Similarly, courts and government officials have also ruled that satanic and Wiccan groups are religious, and that people may now give contributions to those groups and receive the same tax deductions as people who give to Christian churches or Jewish synagogues. [118]

The courts also consider Secular Humanism to be a religion, equivalent under the law to Christianity. [119] What is the primary tenet of the religion of Secular Humanism? It is the conviction that life revolves around man rather than God – it is a man-centered philosophy that excludes God.

Ethical Culture is also a legal religion. [120] It exists to promote ethical values that improve the quality of life for others. For example, it takes credit for establishing the first free kindergarten in eastern America as well as community parks "for play, craft activities, fun and conversation for so many young people." [121] Amazingly, this group which bands together to do good for others is now considered a religion by the Supreme Court, even though the Lion's Club, Red Cross, Boy and Girl Scouts, and dozens of other humanitarian organizations do exactly the same.

Scientology, begun in the 1950s, is now an official religion. [122] Its beliefs are simple: "In Scientology, no one is asked to accept anything as belief or on faith. That which is true for you is what you have observed to be true." [123] The "truth" in this "religion" is individually determined and measured – it is whatever an individual personally picks and chooses to be true. Scientology is often described as a "self-help philosophy," and even though there are dozens of other self-help philosophies and groups across the nation, this one calls itself a "religion" and thus secures additional governmental benefits and constitutional protections.

Universalist Unitarianism (formed in 1961) is now recognized as a legal religion. [124] Interestingly, this may be the most comprehensive "religion" in the world, for it has <u>no</u> fixed set of beliefs or doctrines: "We believe that personal experience, conscience, and reason should be the final authorities in religion, and that in the end religious authority lies not in a book or person or institution but in ourselves. We are a 'non-creedal' religion: we do not ask anyone to subscribe to a creed." [125] Because the primary "doctrine" of this "religion" is that every individual may choose whatever he wants to believe, followers of this "religion" often hold diametrically opposite beliefs on the same issue (e.g., some believe in a Supreme Being of some type but others absolutely do not, etc.); nevertheless, both opposite beliefs are included as part of the *official* beliefs of this legal "religion." (Clearly, every individual in America – or for that matter, in the world – could qualify to be part of this "religion," for all have individual beliefs that stem from their own "personal experience.")

Previously, the beliefs of all of these types of groups were protected by the First Amendment's Free Speech Clause as well as its Assembly Clause (i.e., the right for persons to assemble together into groups of their choice), but **not** by its religion clauses; those clauses existed to protect the truly religious. Now, however, the constitutional protections for the genuinely religious have been expanded to include *every* individual, even the non- and anti-religious, thereby eradicating true religious protections.

Yet, even though all of the above enumerated beliefs (and many others) are now officially considered to be religions (i.e., Christianity is a religion, as is secularism, atheism, universalism, scientology, satanism, etc.), when is the cry "separation of church and state" raised?

That is, do social activists enter public schools at Halloween and demand: "Get those witches down off the wall! Witchcraft is a legal, organized religion recognized by the courts! I demand separation of church and state!" Or do they enter, look around, and insist: "I don't see any prayer here; I don't see any Bible reading here; as a matter of fact, I don't see any religious practice here! That means that the religion of atheism is being practiced here! The religion of secularism is established here! I demand separation of church and state! Get the religions of atheism and secular humanism out of schools!" Such demands are unknown.

So when is the clamor of "separation of church and state" raised? It is heard any time that there is an attempt to involve Judeo-Christian, but not other religious principles – that is, not at Halloween but rather at Thanksgiving, Easter, and Christmas. The complaint is almost universally raised when a Christian expression is present but rarely when the expressions of other religions and beliefs are present. Clearly, then, there is a double standard; today's "separation of church and state" only means that <u>Biblical</u> principles must be kept out of public, not the principles, beliefs, or practices of other religions (or even so-called religions).

Perhaps the clearest demonstration of this fact is evidenced by the United States Court of Appeals for the Ninth Circuit, which has jurisdiction over nine states and fifty-nine million Americans. That federal court ruled that it was <u>not</u> constitutional for public school students to say "under God" in the Pledge of Allegiance [126] but that it <u>was</u> constitutional for public schools to <u>require</u> a three-week general indoctrination to the Islamic faith in which junior-high students – even those who are not Muslim – <u>must</u> pretend

they are Muslims and <u>must</u> offer prayers to Allah; they are further urged to take Islamic names, call each other by those names, wear Islamic garb, participate in Jihad games, and read the Koran during those three weeks. [127] Significantly, that federal court of appeals did not think that requiring Islamic religious activities violated the so-called "separation of church and state" but that voluntarily saying "under God" in the Pledge of Allegiance did.

Similarly, courts have held that classrooms may include materials on Native American religions but that they must remove materials about Christianity. [128] Additionally, Islamic symbols may be publicly displayed at schools during Islamic holidays but Christian symbols may not be displayed during Christian holidays; [129] and schools may accommodate the distinct religious dress and clothing preferences of Muslim but not Christian students. [130] Clearly, "separation of church and state" apparently applies only to Judeo-Christian religious expressions.

Furthermore, because the courts now define religion as anything that a person believes so strongly that it affects the way he behaves, [131] the result is that there will <u>never</u> be a time when *someone's* "religious" beliefs will not be part of public policy. Consequently, the proper question is no longer <u>whether</u> religious beliefs will be part of public policy but rather <u>whose</u> religious beliefs will be part of that policy. Will it be the religious beliefs of atheism, secularism, Islam, Eastern Mysticism, Universalism, self-help Scientology, or a plethora of other religions, creeds, and beliefs? – or will it be the Judeo-Christian beliefs upon which the nation was founded (and which over eight-five percent of Americans still embrace today)? [132]

In short, "separation of church and state" as it exists today is not a teaching of the Founding Fathers or even a historical teaching; however, it *is* the war-cry of the modern secularists and anti-Biblicists. Regrettably, we have ceded much ground in recent years as we have lost our understanding of our own history. We <u>do</u> have a Godly heritage in America, but we've been robbed – robbed by the three percent – by the secularists and what is often an all-too-willing group of public officials and judges who also work to establish secularism across the nation. While there are still numbers of excellent God-fearing public officials and judges at all levels of government who <u>do</u> respect and work to protect our heritage and traditional values, we as voters have become negligent and by our own complacency and lack of investigation into the beliefs of candidates have allowed into public office too many who hold the opposite view.

It is time that Americans relearn their own history and re-familiarize themselves with their own governing documents. As Chief Justice

John Jay recommended:

> Every member of the state ought diligently to read and to study the constitution of his country.... By knowing their rights, they will sooner perceive when they are violated and be the better prepared to defend and assert them. [133]

It is also time for Americans to become reengaged in the civil arena. As John Adams admonished:

> We electors have an important constitutional power placed in our hands. . . . It becomes necessary to every [citizen], then, to be in some degree a statesman and to examine and judge for himself . . . the . . . political principles and measures. Let us examine them with a sober . . . Christian spirit. [134]

In short, it is time for Americans to recover the things given up in recent years – it is time to once again become involved! ■

Endnotes

1. See *Journals of the Continental Congress, 1774 to 1789* (Washington, DC: Government Printing Office, 1904), Vol. I, pp. 26-27, September 6-7, 1774.

2. John Adams, *Letters of John Adams, Addressed to His Wife*, Charles Francis Adams, editor (Boston: Charles C. Little and James Brown, 1841), Vol. I, pp. 23-24, to Abigail Adams on September 16, 1774.

3. Silas Deane, *The Deane Papers: Collections of the New York Historical Society for the Year 1886* (New York: Printed for the Society, 1887), Vol. I, p. 20, September 7, 1774; see also *Letters of the Delegates to Congress*, Paul H. Smith, editor (Washington, DC: Library of Congress, 1976), p. 34.

4. Deane, *Papers*, Vol. I, p. 20, September 7, 1774; see also *Letters of Delegates*, Vol. I, p. 34.

5. John Adams, *Letters*, Vol. I, pp. 23-24, to Abigail Adams on September 16, 1774.

6. *Letters of Delegates*, Vol. I, p. 35, from James Duane's "Notes of the Debates in Congress," September 7, 1774, p. 45, from Samuel Ward's diary for September 7, 1774, p. 55, Samuel Adams to Joseph Warren, September 9, 1774; John Adams, *The Works of John Adams*, Charles Francis Adams, editor (Boston: Little, Brown and Company, 1850), Vol. II, p. 377-378, from his diary entry of September 10, 1774; see also *Letters of Delegates*, Vol. I, p. 60.

7. Benjamin Rush, *Letters of Benjamin Rush*, L. H. Butterfield, editor (Princeton, NJ: American Philosophical Society, 1951), Vol. I, p. 534, to John Adams, February 24, 1790.

8. See *Journals of the Continental Congress* (1904) for June 12, 1775; March 16, 1776; December 11, 1776; November 1, 1777; March 7, 1778; November 17, 1778; March 20, 1779; October 20, 1779; March 11, 1780; October 18, 1780; March 20, 1781; October 26, 1781; March 19, 1782; October 11, 1782; and October 18, 1783.

9. M. E. Bradford, *A Worthy Company* (Marlborough, NH: Plymouth Rock Foundation, 1982), pp. v-vi.

10. From Dictionary.com, s.v. "evangelical."

11. See John Sergeant, *Eulogy on Charles Carroll of Carrollton Delivered at the Request of the Select and Common Councils of the City of Philadelphia, December 31, 1832* (Philadelphia: Lydia R. Bailey, 1833), p. 18. In that day, all major American colleges existed primarily for religious training or the training of ministers and were thus called "seminaries" of learning. (For example, according to John Sergeant – an attorney and a Member of Congress – 29 of the signers of the Declaration "received their education at . . . public seminaries.") In fact, according to the documents of America's major colleges, Harvard's motto was "For Christ and the Church"; William & Mary existed so that "youth may be piously enacted in good letters and manners and that the Christian faith may be propagated"; Yale told its students, "the great end of all your studies . . . is to obtain the clearest conceptions of Divine things and to lead you to a saving knowledge of God in his Son Jesus Christ"; Princeton required that "every student shall attend worship in the college hall morning and evening"; Dartmouth declared that it was established "for the education and instruction of youths . . . in reading, writing, and all parts of learning which shall appear necessary and expedient for civilizing and Christianizing the children"; Columbia College declared that "no candidate shall be admitted into the College . . . unless he shall be able to render into English . . . the Gospels from the Greek"; etc. Signers of the Declaration attending schools that emphasized a reli-

gious course of instruction included John Adams, Samuel Adams, John Hancock, Robert Treat Paine, Elbridge Gerry, William Ellery, William Williams, and William Hooper from Harvard; Oliver Wolcott, Philip Livingston, Lewis Morris, and Lyman Hall from Yale; Richard Stockton, Benjamin Rush, and Joseph Hewes from Princeton; Thomas Jefferson, Carter Braxton, Benjamin Harrison, and George Wythe from the College of William & Mary; Francis Hopkinson, James Smith, and William Paca from the College of Philadelphia; Thomas Nelson, Thomas Lynch, and Arthur Middleton from Cambridge; Francis Lewis from Westminster; John Witherspoon from the University of Edinburgh; James Wilson from the University of St. Andrews, the University of Glasgow, and the University of Edinburgh; and Charles Carroll of Carrollton from the Jesuit Seminaries of Rheimes and the College de St. Omer; additionally, Thomas McKean and George Read studied under the Rev. Dr. Allison, who later started the College of Philadelphia, and Thomas Heyward received private training that was the equivalent of an education taught in the most respected seminaries (Charles Goodrich, *Lives of the Signers* (New York: William Reed & Co., 1829), p. 441). To learn more about the religious purposes of schools in the Founding Era such as Harvard, Yale, Princeton, *et al.*, see David Barton, *Original Intent: The Courts, the Constitution, & Religion* (Aledo, TX: WallBuilder Press, 2002), pp. 81-85.

12. *The Holy Bible* (Trenton: Isaac Collins, 1791).

13. *The Holy Bible*, Charles Thomson, translator (Philadelphia: Jane Aitken, 1808).

14. *The Holy Bible Stereotype Edition* (London: T. Rutt, 1812).

15. Memorial of Robert Aitken to Congress, 21 January 1781, obtained from the National Archives, Washington, DC; see also the introduction to *The Holy Bible As Printed by Robert Aitken and Approved & Recommended by the Congress of the United States of America in 1782* (Philadelphia: R. Aitken, 1782) or the New York Arno Press reprint of 1968; this Bible also referred to as the "Bible of the Revolution."

16. *Journals of . . . Congress*, Vol. XIX, p. 91, January 26, 1781.

17. *Journals of . . . Congress*, Vol. XXIII, pp. 572-573, September 12, 1782.

18. *Journals of . . . Congress*, Vol. XXIII, pp. 572-574, September 12, 1782; see also cover page of the "Bible of the Revolution," either the 1782 original or the 1968 reprint by Arno Press.

19. *Journals of . . . Congress*, Vol. XXIII, p. 574, September 12, 1782.

20. W. P. Strickland, *History of the American Bible Society from its Organization to the Present Time* (New York: Harper and Brothers, 1849), pp. 20-21.

21. C. M. Kirkland, *Memoirs of Washington* (New York: D. Appleton & Company, 1870), p. 155; Washington Irving, *The Life of George Washington* (New York: Thomas Y. Crowell & Company, 1855), p. 138.

22. George Washington, *The Writings of George Washington*, John C. Fitzpatrick, editor (Washington, DC: Government Printing Office, 1931), Vol. 1, p. 152, to John Augustine Washington, July 18, 1755.

23. Washington, *Writings*, Vol. 1, p. 152, to John Augustine Washington, July 18, 1755.

24. Samuel Davies, *Religion and Patriotism the Constituents of a Good Soldier* (Philadelphia: J. Buckland, 1756), pp. 11-12.

25. The American Presidency Project, "Calvin Coolidge: Address before the Congress Sitting in Joint Session in the House of Representatives, February 22nd, 1927" (at http://www.presidency.ucsb.edu/ws/?pid=418).

26. Washington, *Writings*, Vol. 28, p. 120, to Lucretia Van Winter, March 30, 1785.

27. George Washington Parke Custis, *Recollections and Private Memoirs of Washington* (New York: Derby & Jackson, 1860), p. 303.

28. Joseph Banvard, *Tragic Scenes in the History of Maryland and the Old French War* (Boston: Gould and Lincoln, 1856), p. 154.

29. John Adams, *Works*, Vol. X, pp. 45-46, to Thomas Jefferson, June 28, 1813.

30. *The Publications of the American Tract Society* (New York: American Tract Society, circa 1823), Vol. I, pp. 191-192, 288; Vol. VIII, pp. 89-99.

31. Paul Leicester Ford, *The New England Primer: A History of its Origin and Development* (New York: Dodd, Mead, and Co., 1897), plate xxiv, following p. 300.

32. Ford, *Primer*, pp. 310, 313.

33. Emily Ellsworth Ford, *Notes on the Life of Noah Webster* (New York: Privately Printed, 1912), p. 532.

34. William H. Seward, *Life and Public Services of John Quincy Adams* (Auburn: Derby, Miller and Company, 1849), pp. 30-31; John Quincy Adams, *Memoirs of John Quincy Adams*, Charles Francis Adams, editor (Philadelphia: J. B. Lippincott & Co., 1874), Vol. I, p. 8; Josiah Quincy, *Memoir of the Life of John Quincy Adams* (Boston: Phillips, Sampson and Company, 1858), p. 3; *Dictionary of American Biography*, s.v. "John Quincy Adams."

35. Seward, *Life and Public Services*, p. 39; Quincy, *Memoir of the Life*, pp. 3-4; *Dictionary of American Biography*, s.v. "John Quincy Adams."

36. George Washington, *The Writings of George Washington*, Jared Sparks, editor (Boston: Russell, Shattuck, and Williams, and Hilliard, Gray and Co., 1836), Vol. XI, p. 188, to Vice-President John Adams, February 20, 1797.

37. John Quincy Adams, *An Oration Delivered Before the Inhabitants of the Town of New-buryport, At Their Request, on the Sixty-First Anniversary of the Declaration of Independence, July 4th, 1837* (Newburyport, MA: Charles Whipple, 1837), pp. 5, 6.

38. William Jay, *The Life of John Jay* (New York: J. & J. Harper, 1833), Vol. II, p. 376, to John Murray, Jr., October 12, 1816.

39. George Washington, *Address of George Washington, President of the United States, and Late Commander in Chief of the American Army. To the People of the United States, Preparatory to His Declination* (Baltimore: George and Henry S. Keatinge, 1796), pp. 22-23.

40. As an indication of this, see the requirements to hold office that were placed by the signers of the Declaration and the Constitution into the state constitutions they penned. For example, the 1776 Delaware constitution – written with the help of Declaration signers George Read and Thomas McKean and Constitution signer John Dickinson – declared: "Every person who shall be chosen a member of either house, or appointed to any office or place of trust ... shall ... make and subscribe the following declaration, to wit: "I, _____, do profess faith in God the Father, and in Jesus Christ His only Son, and the Holy Ghost, one God, blessed for evermore; and I do acknowledge the Holy Scriptures of the Old and New Testament to be given by divine inspiration." Similar pronouncements are also found in the Massachusetts constitution (written with the help of Declaration signers Samuel Adams, John Hancock, Robert Treat Paine, and John Adams, as well as Constitution signer Nathaniel Gorham), the Pennsylvania constitution (which Declaration signers Benjamin Franklin and James Smith helped write), the Maryland constitution (which Declaration signers William Paca, Charles Carroll, and Samuel Chase helped pen), etc.

41. Conseil Constitutionnel, "Les Constitutions de la France" (at http://www.con-seil-constitutionnel.fr/textes/constitu.htm); see also Harvard Law School, "French Legal Research: Constitution" (at http://www.law.harvard.edu/library/services/research/guides/international/france/const.php).

42. Bucknell University, "The History of the Russian Law Codes" (at http://www.departments.bucknell.edu/russian/politics.html).

43. Afghanistan Online, "History" (at http://www.afghan-web.com/history).

44. University of Michigan, "Polskie Konstytucje – Spis Tresci" (at http://www-personal.engin.umich.edu/~zbigniew/Constitutions/index.html).

45. Donald S. Lutz, *The Origins of American Constitutionalism* (Baton Rouge: Louisiana State University Press, 1988).

46. Lutz, *Origins*, pp. 142-143.

47. Lutz, *Origins*, pp. 142-143.

48. Lutz, *Origins*, pp. 142-143.

49. Lutz, *Origins*, p. 141.

50. Richard Ellsworth Day, *Man of Like Passions* (Grand Rapids, MI: Zondervan Publishing House, 1942), pp. 35-37.

51. *Walz v. Tax Commission*, 397 U.S. 664, 676 (1970).

52. *Church of the Holy Trinity v. U. S.*, 143 U.S. 457, 465, 471 (1892).

53. *Vidal v. Girard's Executors*, 43 U.S. 126, 205-206 (1844).

54. *People v. Ruggles*, 8 Johns 545, 547 (1811).

55. *Holy Trinity* at 470-471.

56. Thomas Jefferson, *The Papers of Thomas Jefferson*, Julian P. Boyd, editor (Princeton, NJ: Princeton University Press, 1950), Vol. I, pp. 530-531, "Rough Draft of Jefferson's Resolutions"; Dumas Malone, *Jefferson and his Time, Volume One, Jefferson the Virginian* (Boston: Little, Brown and Company, 1948), pp. 277-278.

57. William Cathcart, *The Baptists in the American Revolution* (Philadelphia: S. A. George & Co., 1876), pp. 12-18; George Bancroft, *History of the United States of America* (Boston: Little, Brown, and Company, 1858), Vol. I, pp. 449-457; Sanford Cobb, *The Rise of Religious Liberty in America* (New York: Johnson Reprint Corporation, 1902, reprint 1970), pp. 112-114, 490; Mark A. Beliles, *Religion and Republicanism in Jefferson's Virginia* (Charlottesville, VA: The Providence Foundation, 1995), pp. 31-32; Isaac Backus, *A History of New England, with Particular Reference to the Denomination of Christians Called Baptists* (Newton, MA: Backus Historical Society, 1871), Vol. II, pp. 94-95.

58. Joseph Belcher, *The Religious Denominations in the United States* (Philadelphia: John E. Potter, 1865), pp. 161-165; James Madison, *The Papers of James Madison*, Robert A Rutland, editor (Chicago: University of Chicago Press, 1973), Vol. VIII, pp. 298-304, "Memorial and Remonstrance"; *Debates and Proceedings in the Congress of the United States* (Washington, DC: Gales and Seaton, 1849), Vol. I, p. 758, James Madison, August 15, 1789; Washington, *Writings*, Vol. 3, pp. 492, 495-496, General Orders, September 14, 1775, Vol. 27, p. 249, to the Ministers, Elders, Deacons, and Members of the Reformed German Congregation of New York, November 27, 1783, Vol. 30, p. 416, reply to the Quakers, [date unknown]; Kate Mason Rowland, *The Life of George Mason* (New York: G. P. Putnam's Sons, 1892), Vol. I, p. 244.

59. See, for example, Jefferson's replies to various Baptist groups: Thomas Jefferson, *The Writings of Thomas Jefferson* (Washington, DC: Thomas Jefferson Memorial Association,

1904), Vol. XVI, pp. 317-321, 363-364, to the members of the Baltimore Baptist Association, October 17, 1808, to the members of the Ketocton Baptist Association, October 18, 1808, to the general meeting of correspondence of the six Baptist associations represented at Chesterfield, Virginia, November 21, 1808, and to the members of the Baptist Church of Buck Mountain in Albemarle, April 13, 1809; etc.

60. Letter of October 7, 1801 from Danbury (CT) Baptist Association to Thomas Jefferson, Thomas Jefferson Papers, Manuscript Division, Library of Congress, Washington, DC.

61. Jefferson, *Writings*, Vol. XVI, pp. 281-282, letter to the Danbury Baptist Association, January 1, 1802.

62. *Reports of Committees of the House of Representatives Made During the First Session of the Thirty-Third Congress* (Washington, DC: A. O. P. Nicholson, 1854), pp. 6, 8-9.

63. *Journal of the House of Representatives, 34th Congress, 1st Session* (Washington, DC: Cornelius Wendell, 1855), p. 354, January 23, 1856.

64. *Reynolds v. U.S.*, 98 U.S. 145, 164 (1878).

65. *Everson v. Board of Education*, 330 U.S. 1, 18 (1947).

66. WorldNetDaily "How 'Marketing of Evil' really works" (at http://www.worldnetdaily.com/news/article.asp?ARTICLE_ID=47885); American Thinker, "How We Will Lose Our Freedom of Speech" (at http://www.americanthinker.com/2006/11/how_we_will_lose_our_freedom_o.html).

67. In a February 7, 2007, Westlaw search on the phrase "respecting an establishment ...," the results were: all state cases = 1,209 cases; all federal cases = 1,469 cases; total cases using the First Amendment phrase "respecting an establishment" = 2,678 cases. In a February 7, 2007, search on the phrase "separation of church and state," the results were: all state cases = 859 cases; all federal cases = 3,149 cases; total cases using the phrase "separation of church and state" = 4,008. First search string was "wall separati** +4 church +2 state" with Wednesday, February 07, 2007 13:07:00 Mountain as the time of the request. Second search string was (respecting +2 establishment +2 religion) (prohibiting +2 free +1 exercise) with Wednesday, February 07, 2007 12:57:00 Mountain as the time of the request.

68. *Engel v. Vitale*, 370 U.S. 421 (1962).

69. *Engel* at 430.

70. *Reed v. van Hoven*, 237 F.Supp. 48 (W.D. Mich. 1965).

71. *Wallace v. Jaffree*, 472 U.S. 38 (1984).

72. See, for example, *Debates in the Several State Conventions on the Adoption of the Federal Constitution* (Washington, DC: Jonathan Elliot, 1836), Vol. IV, pp. 191-192, 198-199; Kate Mason Rowland, *The Life of George Mason* (New York & London: G.P. Putnam's Sons, 1892), Vol. I, p. 244; Joseph Story, *Commentaries on the Constitution of the United States* (Boston: Hilliard & Gray, 1833), Vol. 3, pp. 728, 730; *Reports of Committees*, p. 6, etc.

73. *Abington v. Schempp*, 374 U.S. 203, 220-221 (1963).

74. *Abington v. Schempp*, 374 U.S. 203 (1963) and *Murray v. Curlett*, 374 U.S. 203 (1963).

75. *Abington* at 209.

76. *Lee v. Weisman*, 505 U.S. 577, 636, 643 (1992) (Scalia, J., dissenting).

77. *County of Allegheny v. ACLU*, 492 U.S. 573, 678 (1989) (Kennedy, J., concurring in part and dissenting in part).

78. *McCollum v. Board of Education*, 333 U.S. 203, 237 (1948).

79. *DeSpain v. DeKalb County Community School District*, 384 F.2d 836 (7th Cir. 1967).

80. *Stone v. Graham*, 449 U.S. 39, 42 (1980).

81. John Adams, *A Defence of the Constitution of Government of the United States of America* (Philadelphia: William Young, 1797), Vol. III, p. 217, from "The Right Constitution of a Commonwealth Examined," Letter VI.

82. *Dictionary of American Biography*, s.v. "James Wilson."

83. James Wilson, *The Works of the Honourable James Wilson* (Philadelphia: Bronson and Chauncey, 1804), Vol. I, pp. 104-105, 106.

84. See, for example, John Adams, *Works*, Vol. VI, p. 9; John Quincy Adams, *Letters of John Quincy Adams to His Son on the Bible and its Teachings* (Auburn, NY: James M. Alden, 1850), pp. 61, 70-71; Samuel Adams, *The Writings of Samuel Adams*, Harry Alonzo Cushing, editor (New York: G. P. Putnam's Sons, 1908), Vol. IV, p. 356; Alexander Hamilton, *The Papers of Alexander Hamilton*, Harold C. Syrett, editor (New York: Columbia University Press, 1961), Vol. I, p. 87, from "The Farmer Refuted"; John Jay, *The Correspondence and Public Papers of John Jay* (New York: G. P. Putnam's Sons, 1893), Vol. IV, p. 403-404, to John Murray, Jr., April 15, 1818; Thomas Jefferson, *The Writings of Thomas Jefferson* (Washington, DC: Thomas Jefferson Memorial Association, 1903), Vol. III, p. 228; James Kent, *Commentaries on American Law* (New York: O. Halsted, 1826), Vol. I, p. 7; Rufus King, *The Life and Correspondence of Rufus King* (New York: G. P. Putnam's Sons, 1900), Vol. VI, pp. 276-277, to C. Gore, February 17, 1820; Joseph Story, *Life and Letters of Joseph Story*, William W. Story, editor (Boston: Charles C. Little & James Brown, 1851), Vol. II, p. 8; Zephaniah Swift, *A System of the Laws of the State of Connecticut* (Windham, CT: John Byrne, 1795), Vol. I, pp. 6-7; Noah Webster, *Letters to a Young Gentleman Commencing His Education: To Which is Subjoined a Brief History of the United States* (New Haven: S. Converse, 1823), p. 7; John Witherspoon, *The Works of John Witherspoon* (Edinburgh: J. Ogle, 1815), Vol. IV, p. 95.

85. See, for example, *State v. Mockus*, 113 A. 39, 41 (Me. 1921); *Cason v. Baskin*, 20 So.2d 243, 247 (Fla. 1944) (en banc); *Bertera's Hopewell Foodland, Inc. v. Masters*, 236 A.2d 197, 200-201 (Pa. 1967); *Paramount-Richards Theatres v. City of Hattiesburg*, 49 So.2d 574, 577 (Miss. 1950); *People v. Rubenstein*, 182 N.Y.S.2d 548, 550 (N.Y. Ct. Sp. Sess. 1959); *Stollenwerck v. State*, 77 So. 52, 54 (Ala. Ct. App. 1917) (Brown, P. J., concurring); *Gillooley v. Vaughn*, 110 So. 653, 655 (Fla. 1926) (citing *Theisen v. McDavid*, 16 So. 321, 323 (Fla. 1894)); *Rogers v. State*, 4 S.E.2d 918, 919 (Ga. Ct. App. 1939); *Brimhall v. Van Campen*, 8 Minn. 1 (1858); *City of Ames v. Gerbracht*, 189 N.W. 729, 733 (Iowa 1922); *Sumpter v. State*, 306 N.E.2d 95, 101 (Ind. 1974); *State v. Schultz*, 582 N.W.2d 113, 117 (Wis. Ct. App. 1998); *Ruiz v. Clancy*, 157 So. 737, 738 (La. Ct. App. 1934) (citing *Caldwell v. Henmen*, 5 Rob. 20 (La. 1843)); *Pierce v. Yerkovich*, 363 N.Y.S.2d 403, 414 (N.Y. Fam. Ct. 1974); *Mileski v. Locker*, 178 N.Y.S.2d 911, 916 (N.Y. Sup. Ct. 1958); *Beaty v. McGoldrick*, 121 N.Y.S.2d 431, 432 (N.Y. Sup. Ct. 1953); *Young v. Commonwealth*, 53 S.W. 963, 966 (Ky. Ct. App. 1932); *Ex parte Mei*, 192 A. 80, 82 (N.J. 1937); *Hardin v. State*, 46 S.W. 803, 808 (Tex. Crim. App. 1898); *Schreifels v. Schreifels*, 287 P.2d 1001, 1005 (Wash. 1955); *Barbour v. Barbour*, 330 P.2d 1093, 1098 (Mont. 1958); *Petition of Smith*, 71 F. Supp. 968, 972 (D.N.J. 1947); *S.B. v. S.J.B.*, 609 A.2d 124, 125 (N.J. Super. Ct. Ch. Div. 1992); *Succession of Onorato*, 51 So.2d 804, 810 (La. 1951); *Hollywood Motion Picture Equipment Co. v. Furer*, 105 P.2d 299, 301 (Cal. 1940); *State v. Donaldson*, 99 P. 447, 449 (Utah 1909); *De Rinzie v. People*, 138 P. 1009, 1010 (Colo. 1913); *Addison v. State*, 116 So. 629 (Fla. 1928); *Anderson v. Maddox*, 65 So.2d 299, 301-302 (Fla. 1953); *State v. Gould*, 46 S.W.2d 886, 889-890 (Mo. 1932); *Doll v. Bender*, 47 S.E. 293, 300 (W.Va. 1904) (Dent, J., concurring); *Pennsylvania Co. v. United States*,

214 F. 445, 455 (W.D. Pa. 1914); *Watts v. Gerking*, 228 P. 135, 141 (Or. 1924); *Hosford v. State*, 525 So.2d 789, 799 (Miss. 1988); *People v. Rosen*, 20 Cal.App.2d 445, 448-449, 66 P.2d 1208 (1937); *Pullum v. Johnson*, 647 So.2d 254, 256 (Fla. Dist. Ct. App. 1994); *Weinstock, Lubin & Co. v. Marks*, 42 P. 142, 145 (Cal. 1895); *Chisman v. Moylan*, 105 So.2d 186, 189 (Fla. Dist. Ct. App. 1958); *Swift & Co. v. Peterson*, 233 P.2d 216, 231 (Or. 1951), and others.

86. *Engel v. Vitale*, 370 U.S. 421, 422 (1962).

87. *State Board of Education v. Board of Education of Netcong*, 262 A.2d. 21, 30 (Sup.Ct.N.J. 1947), cert. denied, 401 U.S. 1013.

88. *Abington v. Schempp*, 374 U.S. 203, 213 (1963).

89. *Grigsby v. Reib*, 153 S.W. 1124, 1129-30 (Tex. Sup. Ct. 1913).

90. *Sheffield v. Sheffield*, 3 Tex. 79, 85-86 (Tex. Sup. Ct. 1848).

91. See, for example, *Eikenbury v. Eikenbury et al*, 70 N.E. 837, 838 (Ind. App. 1904); *State v. Musser*, 70 N.E. 837 (1946); *Sheffield v. Sheffield*, 3 Tex. 79, 85-86 (Tex. Sup. Ct. 1848); *Grigsby v. Reib*, 153 S.W. 1124, 1129 (Tex. Sup. Ct. 1913); *First National Bank of Atlanta v. De Loach*, 74 S.E.2d 740, 741 (Ga. App. 1953); *Tijerina v. Botello*, 207 S.W.2d 136, 138 (Tex. Civ. App. – Austin 1947, no writ); *Finn v. Finn*, 185 S.W.2d 579, 582 (Tex. Civ. App. – Dallas 1945, no writ); *Evans v. Ball*, 6 S.W.2d 180, 181 (Tex. Civ. App. – San Antonio 1928, writ dism'd); *Cole v. Cole*, 299 S.W. 924, 926 (Tex. Civ. App. – San Antonio 1927, no writ); *Tanton v. Tanton*, 209 S.W. 429, 430 (Tex. Civ. App. – El Paso 1919, writ dism'd w.o.j.); and others.

92. Washington, *Address . . . Preparatory to His Declination*, pp. 22-23.

93. U.S. Census Bureau, "Statistical Abstract of the United States 2003: No. HS-14: Births to Teenagers and to Unmarried Women: 1940 to 2002" (at http://www.census. gov/statab/hist/HS-14.pdf).

94. See the U.S. Census Bureau's Statistical Abstract of the United States for the years 1980, 1990, 1991, & 2006: "Births To Unmarried Women" and "Legal Abortions By Selected Characteristics."

95. National Campaign to Prevent Teen Pregnancy, "By the Numbers: The Public Costs of Teen Childbearing, October 2006," (at www.teenpregnancy.org/costs/pdf/report/BTN_National_Report.pdf).

96. See, as just one indication, incidents of syphilis: American Sexually Transmitted Diseases Association, "Epidemiology of Syphilis in the United States, 1941-1993: Age distribution of primary and secondary syphilis by gender, United States, 1956, 1979, 1990, and 1993" (at http://www.stdjournal.com/pt/re/std/fulltext.00007435-199601000-00006. htm;jsessionid=GnVJbTLMJX4HyDhv7p6nBTxyfJkJ3GRL9wMWtXVpsfWZnwJpJ-Phy!3145886!-949856145!8091!-1?index=1&database=ppvovft&results=1&count=10&se archid=7&nav=search). There are literally dozens of separate sexually-transmitted diseases that show similar rises to previously unrecorded highs.

97. U.S. Census Bureau, "Statistical Abstract of the United States 2000: No. 72, Live Births, Deaths, Marriages, and Divorces: 1950 to 2003" (at http://www.census.gov/compendia/statab/2006/vital_statistics/vitstat.pdf).

98. NationMaster.com, "People Statistics: Divorce rate by country" (at http://www.nationmaster.com/graph/peo_div_rat-people-divorce-rate); see also DivorceMagazine.com, "World Divorce Statistics" (at http://www.divorcemag.com/statistics/statsWorld.shtml).

99. Single Parent Families (male & female householders total) in 1960 was 5,782,000; by 2006, the number had increased to 18,902,000. Taken from 2007 Statistical Abstract National Data Book, "Table 57. Households, Families, Subfamilies, and Married Couples: 1960 to 2005" (at http://www.census.gov/compendia/statab/tables/07s0057.xls).

100. Unmarried couples living together were 5,840,833 in 2004 (taken from 2007 Statistical Abstract National Data Book, "Table 61. Unmarried-Partner Households By Sex Of Partners: 2004" (at http://www.census.gov/compendia/statab/tables/07s0061.xls); in 1970, the number was 523,000 (taken from 1995 Statistical Abstract National Data Book, "No. 60. Unmarried Couples, by Selected Characteristics: 1970 to 1994" (at http://www. census.gov/prod/1/gen/95statab/pop.pdf).

101. U.S. Department of Education, "National Center for Education Statistics: Table 129, SAT score averages of college-bound seniors, by sex: 1966-67 to 2003-04" (at http://nces. ed.gov/programs/digest/d04/tables/dt04_129.asp).

102. Washington, *Address . . . Preparatory to His Declination*, p. 23.

103. See the U.S. Census Bureau's Statistical Abstract of the United States for the years 1969, 1980, 1990, & 2007: "Crime and Crime Rates By Type."

104. NationMaster.com, "Crime Statistics: Total crimes by country" (at http://www. nationmaster.com/graph/cri_tot_cri-crime-total-crimes).

105. James Madison, *The Papers of James Madison* (Washington, DC: Langtree & O'Sullivan, 1840), Vol. II, p. 985, by Benjamin Franklin, June 28, 1787.

106. *Debates and Proceedings in the Congress of the United States* (Washington, DC: Gales and Seaton, 1834), Vol. I, p. 28, by President George Washington, April 30, 1789.

107. Thomas Jefferson, *Notes on the State of Virginia* (Philadelphia: Matthew Carey, 1794), Query XVIII, p. 237.

108. Washington, *Writings*, Vol. XII, p. 119, October 3, 1789; see also James D. Richardson, *A Compilation of the Messages and Papers of the Presidents* (Published by Authority of Congress, 1897), Vol. I, p. 56, October 3, 1789.

109. Samuel Adams, *Writings*, Vol. IV, p. 189, article signed "Vindex" in *Boston Gazette*, June 12, 1780.

110. Madison, *Papers*, Vol. III, p. 1391, by George Mason, August 22, 1787.

111. See, for example, Samuel Adams, *Writings*, Vol. III, p. 286; Luther Martin, *The Genuine Information Delivered to the Legislature of the State of Maryland Relative to the Proceedings of the General Convention Lately Held at Philadelphia* (Philadelphia: Eleazor Oswald, 1788), p. 57; see also *Debates in the Several State Conventions on the Adoption of the Federal Constitution*, Jonathan Elliot, editor (Washington, DC: Printed for the Editor, 1836), Vol. I, p. 374.

112. Jay, *Life of John Jay*, Vol. II, p. 376, to John Murray, Jr., October 12, 1816.

113. Charles G. Finney, *Lectures on Revivals of Religion* (New York: Fleming H. Revell Company, 1868, first published in 1835), Lecture XV, pp. 281-282.

114. *An American Dictionary of the English Language* (1849), s.v. "religion."

115. *An American Dictionary of the English Language* (1849), s.v. "religion."

116. See *United States v. Seeger*, 380 U. S. 163 (1965) and *Welsh v. United States*, 398 U.S. 333 (1970).

117. See, for example, *Allegheny v. ACLU*, 492 U.S. 573, 590 (1989), "[The Establishment Clause] guarantee[s] religious liberty and equality to the infidel, the atheist, or the adher-

ent of a non-Christian faith such as Islam or Judaism"; *Malnak v. Yogi*, 440 F.Supp. 1285 (D.C.N.J. 1977); *Kaufman v. McCaughtry*, 419 F.3d 678 (7th Cir. 2005).

118. See, for example, *ACLU v. City of Plattsmouth*, 358 F.3d 1020, 1041 (8th Cir. 2004) ("The First Amendment protects not only Christians and Jews, but atheists, animists, pagans, wicca and everyone alike, no matter whether they are inside or outside the religious mainstream."); *Allegheny v. ACLU*, 492 U.S. 573, 590 (1989) (The Establishment Clause "guarantee[s] religious liberty and equality to the infidel, the atheist, or the adherent of a non-Christian faith such as Islam or Judaism"); a number of Wiccan groups have received 501(c)(3) recognition, including Alexandria Temple, Aquarian Tabernacle Church, Correllian Nativist Church, CWPN, Inc. (Connecticut Wiccan and Pagan Network), Coven Oldenwilde, Journal of African American Witches, Wiccans and Pagans, Our Lady of the Woods, Seekers Circle, The First Congregational Church of the Old Religion, The Witches' Voice, Inc., Tucson Area Wiccan\Pagan Network, United Wiccan Church, Wiccan Religious Cooperative of Florida, Inc., etc. Additionally, a number of groups from the Church of Satan have also received 501(c)(3) recognition, including First Church of Satan, Lilith Grotto Church Inc. of the Church of Satan, Temple of Set, etc.; See also Internal Revenue Service, "Search for Charities" (at http://www.irs.gov/charities/article/0,,id=96136,00.html); *Newsweek*, August 21, 1989, p. 4.

119. See, for example, *Torcaso v. Watkins*, 367 U.S. 488, 495 (1961); *Fellowship of Humanity v. County of Alameda*, 315 P.2d 394; *Grove v. Meade Independent School District*, 753 F.2d. 1528 (1985); *Strayhorn v. Ethical Society of Austin*, 110 S.W.3d 458 (Tex. App. Austin 2003, pet. denied); *Malnak v. Yogi*, 592 F.2d 197 (3d Cir. 1979); *Crockett v. Sorenson*, 568 F. Supp. 1422 (1983).

120. *Torcaso v. Watkins*, 367 U.S. 488 (1961); *Washington Ethical Society v. District of Columbia*, 249 F.2d 127 (D.C. Cir. 1957); *Fellowship of Humanity v. County of Alameda*, 315 P.2d 394; *Strayhorn v. Ethical Society of Austin*, 110 S.W.3d 458 (Tex. App. Austin 2003, pet. denied); *Malnak v. Yogi*, 592 F.2d 197 (3d Cir. 1979).

121. American Ethical Union, "A brief history of the Ethical Culture movement" (at http://www.aeu.org/hist1.html).

122. *Church of Scientology Flag Service Organization, Inc. v. City of Clearwater*, 2 F.3d 1514, 1520 (11th Cir. 1993); *Malnak v. Yogi*, 592 F.2d 197 (3d Cir. 1979).

123. Church of Scientology, "Introduction to Scientology" (at http://www.scientology.org/en_US/religion/index.html).

124. *Strayhorn v. Ethical Society of Austin*, 110 S.W.3d 458 (Tex. App. Austin 2003, pet. denied); see also Internal Revenue Service, "Search for Charities" (at http://www.irs.gov/charities/article/0,,id=96136,00.html).

125. Unitarian Universalist Association, "About Unitarian Universalism" (at http://www.uua.org/aboutuu).

126. *Newdow v. U.S. Congress*, 292 F.3d 597 (9th Cir. 2002).

127. WorldNetDaily, "Judicial Jihad: Judge Rules Islamic Education OK in California Classrooms" (at http://www.worldnetdaily.com/news/article.asp?ARTICLE_ID=36118); at District Court, case was *Jonas Eklund v. Byron Union School District*, 2003 U.S. Dist. LEXIS 27152, U.S.D.C. Case No. 02-3004 PJH (N.D.Cal.) filed August 23, 2003; at the Ninth Circuit the case was *Jonas Eklund v. Byron Union School District*, No. 04-15032 (9th Cir.)

filed November 17, 2005 (D.C. No. CV-02-03004-PJH); at the U. S. Supreme Court, it was *Eklund v. Byron Union School District*, 05-1539, cert. denied.

128. *Roberts v. Madigan*, 702 F. Supp. 1505 (D.C. Colo. 1989).

129. Thomas More Law Center, "Law Center Enters Nativity Dispute in Bay Harbor Islands, FL" (at http://www.thomasmore.org/news.html?NewsID=164); St. Petersburg Times, "Symbols of the season causing a spirited stir" (at http://www.sptimes.com/2004/12/04/State/Symbols_of_the_season.shtml); Agape Press, "Florida Woman Demands Equal Treatment for Public Nativity Display" (at http://headlines.agapepress.org/archive/12/112006c.asp); Fox News, "A Big Legal Win for the Baby Jesus in Florida" (at http://www.foxnews.com/story/0,2933,141777,00.html).

130. *Skoros v. City of New York*, No. 04-1229 (2d Cir. Feb. 2, 2006); WorldNetDaily, "Christmas 'ban' prompts Supreme Court petition" (at http://www.wnd.com/news/article.asp?ARTICLE_ID=51652), and "Another student penalized for pro-life shirt" (at http://www.worldnetdaily.com/news/article.asp?ARTICLE_ID=30861); AgapePress, "At Issue: 'Religious Accommodation' in Public Schools" (at http://headlines.agapepress.org/archive/9/afa/292006d.asp); Pacific Justice Institute, "Students Suspended for Expressing Religious Beliefs" (at http://www.pacificjustice.org/resources/news/focusdetails.cfm?ID=PR060502a); *S.H. v. Penn Cambria School District*, No. 3:06-cv-00271-KRG (W.D. Pa. 2007); *M.G. v. Bush and Shenendehowa Central School District*, No. 1:07-cv-00007-LEK-RFT (N.D.N.Y. 2007).

131. See *United States v. Seeger*, 380 U.S. 163 (1965) and *Welsh v. United States*, 398 U.S. 333 (1970).

132. Pew Research Center, "The 2004 Political Landscape" (at http://people-press.org/reports/display.php3?PageID=757) and "The Diminishing Divide. . . American Churches, American Politics" (at http://people-press.org/reports/print.php3?PageID=451); The Barna Group, "Annual Study Reveals America Is Spiritually Stagnant" (at http://www.barna.org/FlexPage.aspx?Page=BarnaUpdate&BarnaUpdateID=84) and "American Faith is Diverse, as Shown Among Five Faith-Based Segments" (at http://www.barna.org/FlexPage.aspx?Page=BarnaUpdate&BarnaUpdateID=105); City University of New York, "Graduate Center: American Religious Identification Survey, 2001" (at http://www.gc.cuny.edu/faculty/research_studies/aris.pdf); Adherents.com, "Largest Religious Groups in the United States of America" (at http://www.adherents.com/rel_USA.html) and "Gallup Polling Data over Last Ten Years" (at http://www.adherents.com/rel_USA.html – gallup); Harris Interactive, "Large Majority of People Believe They Will Go to Heaven" (at http://www.harrisinteractive.com/harris_poll/index.asp?PID=167); ABCNews.com, "Poll: Most Americans Say They're Christian; Varies Greatly From the World at Large" (at http://abcnews.go.com/sections/us/DailyNews/beliefnet_poll_010718.html); American Public Media, "A Look at Americans and Religion Today" (at http://speakingoffaith.publicradio.org/programs/godsofbusiness/galluppoll.shtml); The Gallup Poll, "Focus On Christmas" (at http://poll.gallup.com/content/default.aspx?ci=14410&pg=2); Baylor University, "American Piety in the 21st Century" (at http://www.baylor.edu/content/services/document.php/33304.pdf).

133. Jay, *Correspondence*, Vol. I, pp. 163-164, from his Charge to the Grand Jury of Ulster County, September 9, 1777.

134. John Adams, *The Papers of John Adams*, Robert J. Taylor, editor (Cambridge, MA: Belknap Press, 1977), Vol. I, p. 81, from "'U' to the *Boston Gazette*," August 29, 1763.

Also Available from WallBuilders

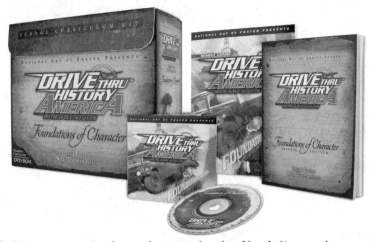

A history curriculum that unabashedly delivers the truth!
Drive Through History America
written by David Barton & presented by award-winning actor Dave Stotts

Visit our website for other great resources!

800-873-2845 • www.wallbuilders.com